Welcome to 2013 a[...]ut

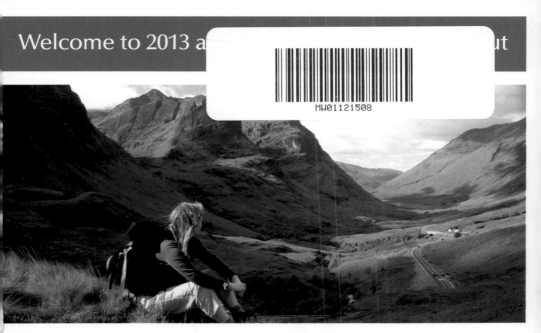

Thank you for being a member of the National Trust for Scotland. This year's member's guide provides you with a wealth of inspiration to ensure that you can make the most of your membership and enjoy great days out all year round.

2013 has been named 'Year of Natural Scotland' and we're using this as an opportunity to celebrate the spectacular countryside, estates and gardens that we care for. Whether you enjoy walking through the dramatic landscape of Glencoe, discovering rare plants and flowers in our world-class gardens like Inverewe in Wester Ross or at Theave Estate in Dumfries and Galloway, or trying out some of our ranger activities across Scotland, we have hundreds of ways to enjoy the great outdoors! Find out more by visiting www.nts.org.uk/natural.

If you're looking for a unique place to stay to experience some of our fantastic places for a wee bit longer then why not look into our self catering properties at www.nts.org.uk/holidays.

Keep in touch with us throughout the year by reading the new-look *Scotland in Trust* magazine or by signing up for our e-newsletter at www.nts.org.uk. For the social media savvy, you can follow us on Twitter or become our friend on Facebook – a great way of telling us about your experiences too!

Year of Natural Scotland 2013

Contents

Appreciation of other funders

The National Trust for Scotland gratefully acknowledges the financial support for conservation projects throughout Scotland provided by our principal funding partners: the Scottish Government; the European Union; Historic Scotland; Scottish Natural Heritage; the Heritage Lottery Fund and the National Heritage Memorial Fund. Receipt of financial assistance from local authorities, local enterprise companies and other companies, trusts and individuals is also gratefully acknowledged. Details are provided in the Trust's Annual Review and Accounts, which are available on request.

The National Trust for Scotland for Places of Historic Interest or Natural Beauty is a charity registered in Scotland, Charity Number SC 007410

Search by category of properties

CASTLES AND GREAT HOUSES
75	Alloa Tower
57	Brodick Castle
117	Brodie Castle
36	Broughton House
90	Castle Fraser
91	Craigievar Castle
93	Crathes Castle
51	Culross Palace
61	Culzean Castle
94	Drum Castle
53	Falkland Palace
95	Fyvie Castle
44	The Georgian House
45	Gladstone's Land
96	Haddo House
73	The Hill House
54	Hill of Tarvit Mansionhouse
65	Holmwood
46	House of the Binns
88	House of Dun
54	Kellie Castle
78	Menstrie Castle
49	Newhailes
69	Pollok House
123	Strome Castle
39	Threave

THE GREAT OUTDOORS
111	Balmacara Estate
81	Ben Lawers National Nature Reserve
72	Ben Lomond
123	Black Hill
57	Brodick Country Park
105	Burg, Isle of Mull
90	Castle Fraser Estate
111	Corrieshalloch Gorge National Nature Reserve
82	Craigower
93	Crathes Estate
61	Culzean Country Park
78	Dollar Glen
94	Drum Estate
112	Falls of Glomach
103	Glencoe & Dalness
58	Goatfell
37	Grey Mare's Tail Nature Reserve
83	The Hermitage
115	Inverewe Estate
84	Killiecrankie
112	Kintail & Morvich
97	Leith Hall Estate
84	Linn of Tummel
98	Mar Lodge Estate
88	Montrose Basin Nature Reserve
99	Pitmedden Estate
37	Rockcliffe
42	St Abb's Head National Nature Reserve
39	Threave Estate
123	Tighnabruaich Viewpoint
113	Torridon
123	Venniehill
113	West Affric

GARDENS
71	Arduaine Garden
81	Branklyn Garden
57	Brodick Castle
117	Brodie Castle
36	Broughton House
90	Castle Fraser
72	Crarae Garden
93	Crathes Castle
51	Culross Palace
61	Culzean Castle
94	Drum Castle
53	Falkland Palace
95	Fyvie Castle
72	Geilston Garden
64	Greenbank Garden
96	Haddo House
41	Harmony Garden
73	The Hill House
54	Hill of Tarvit
65	Holmwood
88	House of Dun
46	Inveresk Lodge Garden
115	Inverewe Garden
54	Kellie Castle
97	Leith Hall
47	Malleny Garden
79	The Pineapple
99	Pitmedden Garden
69	Pollok House
41	Priorwood Garden
39	Threave

HISTORIC SITES
77	Bannockburn
119	Culloden
103	Glencoe
101	Glenfinnan Monument
84	Killiecrankie

ISLANDS
123	Bucinch & Ceardach
105	Canna
122	Fair Isle
106	Iona
106	Mingulay, Berneray & Pabbay
123	Murray Isles
37	Rough Island
109	St Kilda World Heritage Site
123	Shieldaig Island
107	Staffa National Nature Reserve
122	Unst & Yell

HISTORIC BURGHS
51	Culross
82	Dunkeld
53	Falkland

FAMOUS SCOTS
58	Bachelors' Club
87	Barrie's Birthplace
36	Broughton House
59	Robert Burns Birthplace Museum
36	Thomas Carlyle's Birthplace
61	Culzean Castle
66	David Livingstone Centre
44	The Georgian House
96	Haddo House
73	The Hill House
65	Holmwood
46	House of the Binns
88	House of Dun
120	Hugh Miller's Birthplace Cottage & Museum
62	Souter Johnnie's Cottage

SOCIAL & INDUSTRIAL HERITAGE
86	Angus Folk Museum
86	Barry Mill
59	Robert Burns Birthplace Museum
45	Gladstone's Land
120	Hugh Miller's Birthplace Cottage & Museum
79	Moirlanich Longhouse
99	Museum of Farming Life, Pitmedden
65	National Museum of Rural Life
47	Preston Mill & Phantassie Doocot
42	Robert Smail's Printing Works
62	Souter Johnnie's Cottage
67	The Tenement House
67	Weaver's Cottage

Many properties are open all year, either all or some of the winter months. Check individual property entries for further details or visit www.nts.org.uk for information about special seasonal events. For a list of island properties, which by their very nature are open all year, please see page 3.

Dumfries & Galloway

Broughton House (garden only), Kirkcudbright

Grey Mare's Tail Nature Reserve, near Moffat

Rockcliffe, near Dalbeattie

Threave Garden and Estate, including Visitor Centre, Castle Douglas

Scottish Borders

Priorwood Garden, Dried Flower Shop and gift shop, Melrose

St Abb's Head National Nature Reserve, near Coldingham

Edinburgh & the Lothians

House of the Binns (estate only), Linlithgow

Inveresk Lodge Garden, Musselburgh

Malleny Garden, Balerno

Newhailes (estate only), Musselburgh

The Georgian House, Edinburgh

Fife

Royal Burgh of Culross (Trust buildings closed)

Falkland Palace gift shop, near Cupar

Hill of Tarvit (estate only), near Cupar

Kellie Castle (estate only), Pittenweem

Ayrshire & Arran

Brodick Country Park and Goatfell, Arran

Robert Burns Birthplace Museum, Alloway

Culzean Country Park, Maybole

Greater Glasgow & Clyde Valley

Greenbank Garden, Glasgow

David Livingstone Centre, Blantyre

National Museum of Rural Life, East Kilbride

Pollok House and Country Park, Glasgow

Argyll, Bute & Loch Lomond

Arduaine Garden, near Oban

Ben Lomond

Crarae Garden, Inveraray

Central Scotland

Bannockburn (site only)

Dollar Glen, Dollar

The Pineapple grounds, near Falkirk

Perthshire

Ben Lawers National Nature Reserve

Craigower, near Pitlochry

Dunkeld, Ell Shop

The Hermitage, near Dunkeld

Killiecrankie, near Pitlochry

Linn of Tummel, near Pitlochry

Angus

House of Dun grounds, Montrose

Aberdeen & Grampian

Castle Fraser grounds, near Inverurie

Craigievar Castle grounds, Alford

Crathes Castle, Garden and Estate, Banchory

Drum Castle grounds, near Banchory

Fyvie Castle grounds, near Turriff

Haddo House grounds, near Ellon

Leith Hall grounds, near Huntly

Mar Lodge Estate, Braemar

Pitmedden Garden grounds, Ellon

Lochaber

Glenfinnan Monument (site only)

Glencoe Visitor Centre and site

Ross-shire

Balmacara Estate and Woodland Walks

Corrieshalloch Gorge National Nature Reserve

Falls of Glomach

Kintail and Morvich

Torridon

West Affric

Inverewe Garden & Estate, Poolewe

Inverness, Nairn, Moray & the Black Isle

Brodie Castle grounds, near Forres

Culloden Battlefield and Visitor Centre,
near Inverness

Help us to protect and conserve

We are incredibly proud to care for so much of Scotland's rich heritage, but as a charity we depend on people like you to help us care for it.

When you make a donation to the National Trust for Scotland you will help us protect and conserve everything in our care for future generations. Thanks to the generosity of donors we have been able to realise some amazing conservation projects.

Every year we protect Scotland's mountain landscapes from erosion by repairing upland paths at places like Glencoe, Mar Lodge and Torridon. We can only achieve this thanks to generous donations to the Footpath Fund (for more information visit www.nts.org.uk/footpathfund). We have also been able to continue our volunteer education programme, Community Partnerships, where young people who are disengaged with school, and other isolated community groups, are given the opportunity to experience outdoor environments to which they might not otherwise have had access (for more information call 0844 493 2438).

Here's how you can help the National Trust for Scotland:

Call 0844 493 2100 or email development@nts.org.uk to join our Appeals mailing list; you will receive information about our fundraising activities and latest conservation projects.

Give a gift donation to a friend or loved one by visiting www.nts.org.uk/Donate/Gift.

Contact us to receive information on how to remember us in your will. We rely on legacy support to carry out important conservation work. Email legacy@nts.org.uk or call 0844 493 2596.

Donate online at www.nts.org.uk/Donate, call 0844 493 2100, or write to us at Fundraising Department, Hermiston Quay, 5 Cultins Road, Edinburgh EH11 4DF.

The National Trust for Scotland is proud to welcome visitors from both home and overseas. Now visitors from the USA and Canada can continue to support our work and keep up-to-date with our activities through our two dedicated foundations.

Canadian National Trust for Scotland Foundation
Suite 1555
1500 West Georgia Street
Vancouver, BC
Canada V6G 2Z6
Email: iferguson@nts.org.uk
Telephone: 1.604.880.6233

National Trust for Scotland Foundation USA
45 School Street, 3rd Floor
Boston MA 02108
USA
Email: mail@ntsusa.org
Telephone: 617-227-7500

We are a conservation charity that protects and promotes Scotland's natural and cultural heritage for present and future generations to enjoy. Our core purposes are conservation, access and education, through which we provide enjoyment. We depend on your support, whether it is by sponsorship, volunteering, making a donation or remembering us in your Will.

Become a volunteer

Volunteers give enormous help to the Trust and there are many openings throughout the organisation for people to get involved. Working in a voluntary capacity can suit people of all ages who wish to extend their interests, meet new people or learn new skills.

Help bring our properties to life!
Many of our historic buildings and battlefields would simply not be open to the public without the enthusiasm and support of our volunteer guides. By becoming a volunteer guide you will learn about the history of your chosen property and get to see behind the scenes as well. You'll have the excitement of passing Scotland's stories on to other people and the knowledge that you are contributing to the preservation and promotion of Scotland's heritage.

The National Trust for Scotland also has other volunteering opportunities across the country – from helping in our heritage gardens to assisting in our shops.

To find out more about how you can help the Trust through volunteering please have a look at our website – www.nts.org.uk/volunteering. There you can read about volunteer stories, get in touch with the department or search for current volunteer opportunities throughout the organisation.

For further information please contact: The Volunteer Office, Hermiston Quay, 5 Cultins Road, Edinburgh EH11 4DF; tel 0844 493 2402.

Community partnerships – a place for everyone
We firmly believe that the National Trust for Scotland is for everyone. Our Outdoor Action Community Partnerships programme provides opportunities for people and communities from a wide range of backgrounds to engage with the Trust. We aim to encourage everyone to learn about, enjoy and value Scotland's natural and cultural heritage. Our partners are national and local organisations who work with hard-to-reach communities.

For further information please contact: Community Partnerships, Hermiston Quay, 5 Cultins Road, Edinburgh EH11 4DF; tel 0844 493 2438.

Each year a fantastic 3,000 volunteers assist the Trust with events, specialist advice, and the conservation and preservation of properties all over Scotland.

Our volunteers are as diverse as the people of Scotland, with everyone contributing and making a difference. There is something to suit everyone.

Have a look at our website for news, opportunities and updates on volunteering with the National Trust for Scotland: www.nts.org.uk/volunteering

Conservation volunteer opportunities

Weekend and day projects

You can join one of our five Conservation Volunteers groups based in Glasgow, Edinburgh, Aberdeen, Perth and Inverness. These dedicated volunteers take part in day and weekend projects across Scotland throughout the year, doing practical countryside conservation work such as woodland management and footpath repair. Transport, food and accommodation are provided on residential projects. However, on day projects you need to bring a packed lunch and the project CV leader will bring tea, coffee and biscuits. No experience is necessary but you should be over 18, reasonably fit and enjoy working outdoors.

There are many benefits of becoming a registered Conservation Volunteer, which costs a one-off fee of £25 to non-Trust members. These include exploring new places and making new friends; working on the 'frontline', alongside our expert property staff; learning new skills and in doing so helping to conserve Scotland's countryside.

Once registered, volunteers can sign up for projects and also benefit from a year's free membership of the National Trust for Scotland.

For a copy of one of the groups' seasonal work programmes, or to find out more about outdoor Conservation Volunteers, visit www.nts.org.uk/ Volunteering/Outdoor or call 0844 493 2589.

Working holidays

Thistle Camps are working holidays which help in the conservation and management of countryside properties. They run between March and October and take place in magnificent surroundings throughout Scotland.

The work is diverse, rewarding, stimulating and fun and can include footpath repair/construction, fencing, archaeological surveys and excavations, environmental art projects, bat surveys, gardening, barn building training courses, and woodland management. Thistle camps are a wonderful opportunity to 'give something back' and can also contribute to the residential part of the Duke of Edinburgh Gold Award.

We also run Trailblazers Thistle Camps for 16 and 17 year-olds. Trailblazers combine essential conservation work with adventure-type activities such as sea-kayaking, gorge-walking or learning survival skills.

All work will be fully explained and techniques demonstrated. Appropriate skills are welcome but not essential, as all camps are supervised by an experienced leader and property staff.

Camps start at £70. There are reduced rates for students, unwaged and retired people, and prices vary depending on the time of year and the duration of the camp.

For further details, online booking, or to download a copy of the Thistle Camps brochure, please visit www.nts.org.uk/thistlecamps. Or contact Thistle Camps, Hermiston Quay, 5 Cultins Road, Edinburgh EH11 4DF; tel 0844 493 2590.

Each year, around 800 dedicated and enthusiastic volunteers carry out practical conservation work, completing up to 120 projects.

Have you considered volunteering through your work? See page 18 for more information.

Countryside and wildlife

The Trust cares for 76,000 hectares of Scotland's finest countryside. We are the third largest landowner in Scotland and the largest managing the land for conservation purposes. It includes mountains at the heart of both National Parks, 7 National Nature Reserves, 27 European Natura-2000 sites, 45 Sites of Special Scientific Interest, and many Scheduled Ancient Monuments – a huge responsibility and one that we take very seriously.

Keeping watch

Much of the wildlife and natural habitats we look after require little intervention – just a wary eye on their continuing good health. We monitor rare plants at Ben Lawers and Grey Mare's Tail, keep watch on the nests of peregrines and eagles, and carry out surveys of the fauna, flora and vegetation communities.

Action

We are working to restore native woodlands at Mar Lodge Estate, Glencoe, Torridon and Balmacara; wetlands at Threave, Goatfell and Montrose Basin; as well as helping to increase corncrake numbers at Canna, Staffa and Iona and black grouse at Ben Lomond and Mar Lodge Estate.

Balance

Much of our lower ground is farmed by agricultural tenants who need to continue to make a living from the land, therefore a balance is encouraged to benefit wildlife and archaeology without damaging the farmers' income. Such schemes have been put in place at House of Dun, Iona and Balmacara.

Access

Over two million people visit us each year. Our properties include one-sixth of all Munros (mountains over 3,000ft) and attract huge numbers of hill walkers. To protect the fragile soils from erosion we have restored over 100km of upland footpaths, including removing high altitude vehicle tracks. In the lowlands, we provide attractive walks and viewing hides.

Ranger service

Helping visitors to understand the wildlife and countryside around them is a major focus of our effort. Our staff of 60 rangers give over 500 guided walks a year and introduce some 20,000 schoolchildren to the great outdoors. In addition, we develop interpretative displays and guidebooks for a wider audience.

All this work is designed to pass on the wonderful natural heritage and landscapes in the Trust's care in good condition. We hope that you will enjoy your visit.

The Trust's countryside management programme is supported by Scottish Natural Heritage.

We care for 76,000 hectares of Scotland's finest countryside. This includes mountains at the heart of both National Parks, 7 National Nature Reserves, 27 European Natura-2000 sites, 45 Sites of Special Scientific Interest, and many Scheduled Ancient Monuments.

Gardens in trust

There are 70 gardens and designed landscapes connected with Trust properties, ranging from small gardens associated with museum properties, landscaped amenity sites at battlefields and visitor centres, to the bigger and more important ornamental gardens and large designed landscapes that complement the settings of the great castles and houses of Scotland. Almost every style of Scottish garden history is represented – from late medieval at Culross Palace, through 18th-century Picturesque at Culzean, Victorian formality at Haddo and House of Dun to the early 20th-century horticultural masterpieces at Arduaine, Branklyn, Crarae and Inverewe, as well as the modern creations at Falkland Palace, Inveresk Lodge and Priorwood.

Gardens, whether large or small, their policies and wider designed landscapes are living works of art comprising a series of characteristics including land form, soils, microclimate, availability and use of plant material, and the influence of people through personal taste and changes in fashion. These, together with many other factors, are managed on behalf of the Trust by just over 100 full-time gardeners and support staff who guide the day-to-day conservation management of the gardens to ensure they are presented to the highest standards.

The Trust operates a gardener training programme, known as the *School of Heritage Gardening*, which aims to provide a range of training opportunities at a number of key gardens. For over 50 years the Trust has run a School of Practical Gardening at Threave, and in recent years garden apprenticeships have also been offered at Inverewe, Kellie Castle, Pitmedden and Geilston, with other short-term placements at Castle Fraser, Crathes Castle, Leith Hall, Greenbank and Drum Castle gardens.

With more than 283 hectares under intensive cultivation, and supporting over 80,000 plants of which there are 13,500 different sorts, our gardens are internationally renowned for their plant collections. Geographical and climatic diversity, such as the Gulf Stream's effect on west coast gardens, provide conditions for the growth of remarkable, often unique, collections. Look out for special events such as garden walks, talks, lectures, demonstrations, apple days, wildlife events, special plant sales, musical performances and much more. Enjoy a great day out and help celebrate Scotland's very special garden heritage!

Scotland's Gardens

The Trust is indebted to Scotland's Gardens for its continued support of the Trust's garden activities through an annual donation. Each year over 350 Scottish gardens, most of them privately owned, are opened to the public just one day a year under the Scotland's Gardens banner. In addition to the Trust, Scotland's Gardens also supports the Queen's Nursing Institute (Scotland) and Maggie's Cancer Caring Centres, among others.

Details of opening times for Scotland's Gardens days are listed in their annual handbook, available from mid-February at Trust shops and from Scotland's Gardens, 42a Castle Street, Edinburgh EH2 3BN.
Tel 0131 226 3714,
www.gardensofscotland.org

The Trust are holders of 17 Plant Heritage (NCCPG) National Plant Collections

Collections & conservation

Collections

The Trust is responsible for the care of tens of thousands of artefacts, from great works of art to humble domestic items, nearly all of which are displayed in their original context. By 'original context' we mean the historic interiors of the castles and great houses owned by the Trust, which might include original wooden panelling, decorative paint schemes on the walls or ceilings, as well as ornate plasterwork. It is seeing collections in such settings that makes a visit to a Trust house or castle so different from a visit to a museum.

How we care for the collections

The primary means by which the Trust cares for its collections, as well as the historic interiors in which they are presented, is through the delivery of 'preventive conservation'. This means identifying and managing the 'threats' to our collections, whether those threats are to a magnificent library full of books, a fragile gilded mirror, or original carpets and curtains.

What are the potential threats?

Inappropriate levels of light, temperature and humidity can wreak havoc on our collections and the rooms they are in, as can pests in the shape of woodworm or moths. Other threats are the risk or fire or theft, as well as the impact of visitors within a property.

How you can help

Understanding and appreciating the Trust's philosophy of care to its collections are the keys to helping you play your part.

Why are the blinds drawn?

Light levels must be kept low, as light causes colours to fade and fabrics and paper to become weak and brittle. Historically, housekeeping staff would have maintained a strict daily regime of keeping blinds drawn and shutters closed, as well as covering other items of furniture, when rooms were not in use.

Why can't I touch things?

One person touching a curtain or the back of an upholstered chair may not do much harm, but just imagine the consequences if everyone were to do so. Picture frames are another example; most are decorated with beautiful gold leaf, and inevitably dust falls to the bottom edge of the frame. In the past, rubbing a duster on the frame has worn away the gold, so we now use soft pony-hair brushes to gently brush the dust directly into the nozzle of a vacuum cleaner.

What can we do to help protect the floors and carpets?

Our floors take a pounding from thousands of feet every year. Visitor routes, with roped walkways and protective druggets placed on top of carpets, help us to manage the impact of all those feet, but shoes themselves can cause considerable damage. We therefore ask that heels are larger than 20mm square in order to avoid damaging floors.

The Trust conserves and cares for some of the finest built structures that make up Scotland's unique architectural heritage.

By visiting Trust properties you are showing that you care about preserving our heritage for future generations of visitors to enjoy.

Little Houses Improvement Scheme

Imagine a Trust property and you may well think of a castle, a grand mansion, a stunning garden or a mountain. However, the Trust also protects some of Scotland's finest vernacular architecture through its Little Houses Improvement Scheme (LHIS). The LHIS acquires properties that are neglected or at risk, repairs them and then sells them on, promoting the renewal and regeneration of once redundant buildings and communities. The scheme also applies its expertise on occasions to identifying solutions to redundant Trust buildings.

In 2011 we completed an ambitious scheme in the centre of Peterhead – the repair and adaptation of a group of Georgian townhouses in the heart of the old burgh to form much-needed housing for people with learning and physical disabilities. Over 18 months the buildings were transformed from their previously derelict and ruinous state to homes of great character and quality, befitting their position in the centre of the Peterhead Outstanding Conservation Area. The project has spearheaded the Conservation Area Regeneration Scheme, inspiring others to help preserve the town's rich architectural heritage. In addition, the LHIS engaged with the future residents, community groups, schools, and local artists and craftsmen to deliver a programme of activities celebrating Peterhead's heritage.

While the LHIS develops projects and seeks out new opportunities, previously completed projects continue to win accolades. In 2012 the Peterhead project received six awards, in recognition of the exemplary conservation work of the Trust through the LHIS. The awards included the RICS Scotland Regeneration Award, the Scottish Homes Award Community Partnership of the Year, and the best cultural event NE Scotland for the drama production about the project, *The Hoose*.

2012 saw the assessment and development of projects from South Ayrshire to Shetland, with at least one project – the repair of a pair houses in Culross – programmed to start on site in 2013.

The story of the Trust's championing of small historic properties is told in *Little Houses* by Diane Watters and Miles Glendinning, published by RCAHMS, and available from most Trust shops.

Restoring buildings and communities together.

Members' Centres and Friends Groups

Join your local Members' Centre or Friends Group
With support groups throughout Scotland, as well as London and Cambridge, members have the opportunity to become more involved with the Trust and the properties they feel closest to.

The details
Members get together through a programme of social, cultural and fundraising events including lectures, walks, day outings and weekend trips. Many of the groups also support the Trust through volunteer guiding, conservation work and membership recruitment, as well as getting involved with events at properties. They also raise thousands of pounds annually for the Trust's work at local and national level.

Most groups are independently registered charities in their own right, who are supported by a co-ordinator in the Membership & Customer Services Department. If you would like more information on how to join your local group, call 0844 493 2565 and you will be put in contact with the appropriate group secretary. Details of events are published with *Scotland in Trust* magazine twice a year.

Get more from your membership.

Gift membership & Discover tickets

Gift membership

If you are a member of the National Trust for Scotland you will already know about the many benefits you enjoy – why not let someone else enjoy the same benefits and privileges with your compliments? A Trust membership could be just the thing for the 'person who has everything'.

When gifting a membership, the Trust can administer it either as a one-off gift or, if you wish, it can be set up as a continuing gift which will carry on every year until you tell us to stop. We can provide you with the full 'Welcome' pack, so that you can gift wrap it and hand it over personally. Alternatively, we can personalise a gift card for you and send it together with the pack straight to the new member. The choice is yours.

To find out more, or to start the process for someone you wish to share the Trust's treasures with, call the Customer Services Centre on 0844 493 2116 quoting reference 'PG'.

Discover tickets

Discover tickets are the perfect way for your friends and family, who are not National Trust for Scotland members, to enjoy visits to as many Trust properties as they like over a period of 3, 7 or 14 days. They are available as family or adult tickets and can be converted to Trust membership at any of our staffed properties. Tickets can be purchased at any staffed property or by contacting the Customer Services Centre on 0844 493 2100.

Get your business involved in conservation

Corporate Challenge

Corporate Challenge offers companies the chance to take an active role in conserving important and fragile landscapes across Scotland, while developing their staff teams in a completely new and challenging environment. Groups are encouraged to demonstrate various team skills including leadership, good communication, delegation and problem solving through practical conservation work.

If your business is keen to develop their staff and increase their community involvement, then visit our Corporate Challenge website at www.nts.org.uk/volunteering/Corporate. For more information email us at corporatechallenge@nts.org.uk or call 0844 493 2588.

Corporate hospitality

Need a spectacular venue to host an important corporate function? Contact the Customer Services Centre on 0844 493 2111 to make your event happen.

Become a Corporate Partner or Sponsor

We hold an exciting and diverse range of projects and events throughout the year that your company can get involved in. Working closely with your organisation, we will maximise the benefit to you and develop a package tailored to your specific needs. Your company will also experience positive PR and can fulfil essential corporate social responsibility criteria by playing your part in conserving Scotland's natural and cultural heritage.

As a charity we rely on our members to support our work. There are various options available to suit your organisation, which are flexible and can be tailored to meet your company's needs. You will receive unique staff benefits and opportunities while supporting Scotland's natural and cultural heritage.

If you have a promotional idea of your own or would like more information on any of our corporate opportunities, please contact our Corporate Business Development Manager by email at development@nts.org.uk or call 0844 493 2458.

Learning opportunities

Teachers
Our Learning Services staff are always available to give advice, help prepare visits and assist with project work and topic-based learning. The 3-18 curriculum is particularly well catered for and most of our events and programmes mesh neatly with Curriculum for Excellence guidelines. Many of our activities are ideally suited to cross-curricular work and you will be surprised how many outcomes are covered.

Outdoors
From Arran to Crathes, and Newhailes to Culzean, we can offer unique learning opportunities. The great diversity of our countryside properties, combined with our knowledgeable and dedicated Countryside Ranger Service, allows you and your pupils to move your classroom outdoors. Environmental education, climate change and many other topics and practical activities guarantee that you will have a rewarding and fun day out.

Indoors
Our castles and historic houses provide excellent opportunities if you are studying topics such as the built environment or 'People in the Past'. There are costumes to be worn, poems to be written, and works of art to be created – all that you need is your creativity!

We offer programmes which support many areas of the curriculum at a variety of levels. Students of tourism, ecology and environmental studies will also find our properties a useful resource. Many properties are also excellent venues for creative arts and workshop-based activities.

Transport subsidy
We may be able to offer a transport subsidy to school groups towards the cost of coach hire when visiting Trust properties. Check www.ntslearning.org.uk or call 0844 493 2106 for further details.

Schools programme
Our schools programme is packed with details of our properties and the learning programmes and opportunities that we offer. It is sent to every school in Scotland, but if you would like to receive a free copy please call 0844 493 2106.

Educational publications
Every property has a Property Information Sheet, which details all the learning opportunities available there. This can be downloaded from our Learning Services website. We also have teaching packs, special Wee Guides for children, and many more resources, details of which can be found on the website.

Educational membership
Many schools find this the most cost-effective way to visit Trust properties. This not only allows a teacher or lecturer a free preliminary tour before each visit, but thereafter it allows the school, college or group free visits to all properties (except Culloden) throughout the year's membership during academic term times. In addition, it entitles reduced price for various special educational events and workshops.

Website
Our website contains a wealth of information for teachers, students and pupils looking for help with projects or planning to visit a Trust property (see www.ntslearning.org.uk). The website has recently been updated and contains many new features and sections, including a suite of virtual tours within some of the Trust's properties.

The Trust offers limitless opportunities to all sectors of education. Primary, secondary, tertiary and community groups are all welcome and specific visits or activities can be arranged to match the requirements of visiting students and groups.

A place for entertaining

For spectacular venues, memories you'll treasure for a lifetime and outstanding customer service at a price you can afford, the National Trust for Scotland is the perfect choice.

For centuries our properties have played host to magnificent feasts and celebrations for the rich and famous. Today they are available to you for private hire and corporate entertaining.

From fairytale weddings and civil ceremonies to champagne receptions and exclusive dinners, for anniversaries, birthdays, christenings and family reunions, we have something to offer everyone.

Across Scotland, we have a host of venues steeped in history, myth and legend. From intimate celebrations to lavish marquee receptions, our castles and stately homes are set in stunning countryside and city locations, surrounded by enchanting gardens and rolling estates.

Whatever the occasion, our chefs and catering partners will create the menu of your choice using only the best Scottish ingredients, whilst our property teams will allow you to relax, comforted that you are in good hands.

Celebrate with us, reassured by the knowledge that you are directly supporting our vital conservation work and helping protect Scotland's natural and cultural heritage for present and future generations to enjoy.

For information on holding your event at a National Trust for Scotland venue call 0844 493 2111 (+44 131 458 0438 from outside the UK), email functions@nts.org.uk or visit www.nts.org.uk

Events for everyone

The National Trust for Scotland organises a wide range of exciting and varied events to suit all ages and interests. From guided walks and nature rambles, to costumed presentations, live music and concerts, outdoor theatre, seasonal festivities, craft and plant fairs, and much more. Our events provide enjoyment but also a chance to learn or to try something new in a variety of unusual and beautiful locations.

If you're planning a trip to one of our sites or simply want to know what's going on this week at your local property, then visit www.nts.org.uk for a more detailed picture. Here you can create your own events list for your favourite properties or for the type of events that you prefer. An extra charge may be made for events, which also applies to Trust members.

To receive regular updates on events visit www.nts.org.uk/events

There are over 60 holiday properties across Scotland for you to choose from, ranging from cottages on Highland country estates to remote crofts on the Isle of Skye, from wings of castles and a shooting lodge in the Cairngorms to apartments in Edinburgh's historic city centre.

High standards

All accommodation is maintained to a high standard and inspected annually under VisitScotland's Quality Assurance Scheme to give you the reassurance of choosing the standard of accommodation you want. Our properties in the Highlands have also joined the Green Tourism Business Scheme, which places an onus on the Trust to run the accommodation in an environmentally sensitive way.

Time and space

Properties sleep between 2 and 15 people, and are available for short breaks as well as full weeks. If you would like to book a Christmas or New Year break, get in touch well before the festive season, since this is a very popular time.

For lovers of the great outdoors

Base Camps are available in more remote areas, such as Brodick, Kintail, Torridon and Canna. They sleep between 8 and 20 and provide basic, comfortable facilities to give you the best start to that energetic day on the hills.

If you would like to receive a copy of our full brochure or wish to check availability, you can do this via our website (www.nts.org.uk) or you can telephone the Holidays Department on 0844 493 2108. We look forward to welcoming you to one of our properties in 2013!

Cultural cruising

This year the National Trust for Scotland celebrates 60 years of cultural cruising. Since the first voyage set sail in 1953, the annual Trust cruises have carried thousands of passengers round Scotland's islands, breathtaking coastlines and beauty spots. Our itineraries change every year and mix little known and rarely visited ports with renowned and popular destinations. The cruises combine unique and interesting routes with excellent service, a friendly and relaxed atmosphere, fascinating lectures, high-quality shore excursions and sophisticated entertainment. All profits from our cruises contribute to the Trust's vital conservation work, including projects connected to its islands and coastlines.

We run two cruises each year: a one-week holiday around the Scottish coastline and islands, with a visit to the remote St Kilda World Heritage Site, and a two-week cruise to some of the most interesting corners of Europe. Past itineraries have taken us to Spitsbergen, the Gulf of Bothnia, Iceland, the Norwegian coastline and St Petersburg. All our cruises sail from and return to Scottish ports.

We charter the beautiful *Quest for Adventure*, which takes just 400 passengers, all of whom will be friends or members of the National Trust for Scotland, evoking a convivial, club-like atmosphere on board. The ship offers the ultimate in comfort and elegance, with outstanding service, delicious food and great facilities.

For full details of our current cruises please contact us on cruises@nts.org.uk, call 0844 493 2457, or visit our website www.culturalcruising.com

Whether your interest lies in sailing, hillwalking, visiting historic houses, castles and distilleries, 'doing' the Edinburgh Festival or enjoying a romantic break in a secluded Gothic lodge, the Trust has something for everyone.

Visitors with disabilities

The Trust warmly welcomes all visitors with physical, sensory and learning disabilities. We recognise that many historic properties and the countryside can present difficulties for people with disabilities. We are continually implementing procedures, changes and extra provision, where possible, to ensure that all our visitors can enjoy a comfortable and enjoyable day out. We do recommend contacting the property in advance for detailed access facilities, and also to check for any temporary constraints that may apply on that day.

While disabled visitors are charged the normal admission price, any necessary companion is admitted free. We welcome all assistance dogs.

Details of disabled access can be found in this Guide in the information panel on each property page.

Member checkpoint

Admission and parking

As a member you are entitled to free entry to all properties owned by the Trust which are open to the public, during normal opening times and under normal opening arrangements. Your membership also allows you free parking. Membership cards are not transferable.

Please bring your current membership card with you, since we regret we can't admit you free of charge without it and admission charges cannot be refunded subsequently. Please display your National Trust for Scotland car sticker, as without it there is a parking charge of £2.

Reciprocal arrangements with other National Trusts

As a member you are granted free or concessionary admission by other National Trusts to properties in Australia, Bahamas, Barbados, Bermuda, Canada, Cayman Islands, Fiji, Guernsey, India, Ireland, Isle of Man, Jamaica, Malaysia, Malta, New Zealand, Virgin Islands and Zimbabwe. For a full list contact the Customer Services Centre on 0844 493 2100.

The National Trust is a separate organisation covering England, Wales and Northern Ireland. Information about their properties is published in the National Trust Handbook, available by emailing enquiries@nationaltrust.org.uk, or at www.nationaltrust.org.uk. Alternatively, write to Membership Department, PO Box 39, Warrington, Cheshire, WA5 7WD.

Members of the National Trust for Scotland are admitted free of charge to National Trust properties in England, Wales and Northern Ireland.

Customer service

Visitor attraction quality assurance
VisitScotland's Quality Assurance Scheme provides an independently verified grading of standards of facilities and services provided at an attraction. Look out for the plaques on your visits.

Customer Services Centre
For any queries you have about opening times, events, or holiday and property information – or even to let us know about your experiences after you have visited one of our properties, please contact the Customer Services Centre. Our aim is to become 'the friendliest organisation in Scotland'. We want your visit to be enjoyable and for you to return to our properties time and time again.

Contact the Customer Services Centre on 0844 493 2100; write to the Customer Services Centre, The National Trust for Scotland, Hermiston Quay, 5 Cultins Road, Edinburgh, EH11 4DF; or email information@nts.org.uk.

The National Trust for Scotland welcomes RNID Typetalk. Please call 18001 493 2100 to contact Customer Services via Typetalk.

RNID Typetalk

Calls to the Trust's Customer Services Centre may be monitored and recorded for training purposes.

Families

Quizzes and trails
The Trust provides a range of facilities for families. Many properties have children's guidebooks or quiz sheets, special trails and other activities permanently on offer to keep young visitors entertained.

Events and clubs
A big feature at many of our properties are Family Fun Days, children's walks and workshops. Extra events are arranged over weekends, school holidays and Bank Holidays. For listings, visit the events pages at www.nts.org.uk. At certain properties, such as Culzean and Newhailes, there are also activity clubs for children. Please call individual properties for more information.

Facilities
In buildings, visitors with small babies are welcome to use front slings, which are often available on loan. Please note that in some of our buildings, because of their fragile interiors, it is not always possible to use baby backpacks, prams and pushchairs, so storage is usually available at the entrance. Baby changing facilities are provided at several properties.

The family symbol is used on the property pages to highlight these facilities.

Dog policy

For many people, bringing their dog with them to a Trust property can enhance the enjoyment of their visit, and exercising their dog may even be the main purpose of their visit. For those with assistance dogs, the visit would be impossible without their dog accompanying them. The Trust has published a policy on dogs at Trust properties, which is available on the website (www.nts.org.uk) or by calling our Customer Services Centre on 0844 493 2100.

In summary:

• all dogs under proper control and accompanied by responsible owners, who clean up after them, will be welcomed at Trust properties;
• assistance dogs (and assistance dogs under training) are allowed full access to all public areas of the property;
• all other dogs are permitted access to public areas of the property, except for buildings open to the public. In the immediate area beside buildings and within the proximity of other visitor facilities, dogs should be under close control;
• only assistance dogs are permitted in walled or enclosed gardens;
• during special events, it will be at the discretion of the organisers as to whether dogs may be permitted. If in doubt, please call to discuss arrangements in advance.

While the welfare of dogs at Trust properties is primarily the responsibility of dog owners, in some instances the Trust will provide facilities, including areas to exercise dogs, provision of dog-waste bins or shaded parking. Please check our website for further details or call the property to discuss arrangements before making a visit.

Further useful information can be found in the Scottish Outdoor Access Code, describing the rights of responsible access enabled by the Land Reform (Scotland) Act 2003 (www.outdooraccess-scotland.com).

Robert Burns Birthplace Museum

A place for eating

For delicious home-made Scottish food, outstanding customer service and exquisite surroundings, nothing compares to a visit to a National Trust for Scotland property.

With 25 tearooms, cafés and restaurants at amazing locations across Scotland, including our 120-cover café at Robert Burns Birthplace Museum in Alloway, we have something to tempt all ages and tastes. Pop in, relax and indulge yourself.

Our exciting new menus offer a wide selection of home baking, delicious home-made soups and wholesome main courses, as well as healthy choices and light snacks, including fairly traded and gluten-free options.

For those of you with a sweet tooth, treat yourself to our mouth-watering home-made cakes and devilish desserts – like Threave's traditional banoffee pie and Culloden's wonderful malteser tiffin and ginger fudge slice.

Our menus change seasonally and vary from property to property, from Scottish hotplate pancakes with Ayrshire bacon and maple syrup at Robert Burns Birthplace Museum, to Highland venison pie at Inverewe Garden. We also try to source locally wherever possible, from Brodick Castle's local Arran produce to Pitmedden's garden preserves – delicious with their home-made scones.

Whether you're a Trust member, paying visitor, volunteer, student, family or grandparent, everyone is welcome! Many of our venues have children's play areas and changing facilities.

Every coffee we make, every cake we bake, we'll be helping you to enjoy your holidays and days out, and you'll be helping us to look after Scotland's heritage. Thank you for your continued support.

Green Tourism Business Scheme

As part of the National Trust for Scotland's commitment to the environment, we participate in the Green Tourism Business Scheme (GTBS). This provides an independent assessment of all aspects of a property's approach to the environment, including issues such as energy use, how we deal with our waste, and where we purchase our food from. Importantly, the GTBS also requires continual improvement.

Almost all our properties which are eligible for the GTBS have now gone through the audit process, and all of those have been granted an award. The property pages in this guide display the GTBS logo and award level for these properties. We are working to ensure that any remaining properties which are eligible for the GTBS also become members of the scheme.

Shops

Why not call into one of our shops and indulge in a little retail therapy?

Our shops stock an extensive range of gifts and souvenirs from Scotland and around the world, so you can be sure that there is something for everyone when you visit. In our shops you will find a wide range of books covering all aspects of Scotland's history and culture, as well as a range of Scottish music titles to get your feet tapping. We stock ranges of beautiful jewellery, sumptuous textiles and luxurious homewares – ideal as a treat either for yourself or a friend, as well as toys and gifts to amuse and inspire our younger visitors. We also sell a variety of food and confectionery products made in Scotland from the finest ingredients.

We support eco-friendly schemes and suppliers, and promote products and ranges with ethical and Fairtrade origins.

You can also visit our online shop at www.nts.org.uk, where you can view some of our ranges from the comfort of your own home. Here you will find a selection of gifts, books and souvenirs suitable for every occasion. With delivery available worldwide, you can help support the Trust no matter where you are.

Whatever you buy, you can be assured that all the proceeds from our shops go towards our vital conservation work. By spoiling yourself, you are also helping to look after Scotland's heritage.

Plant sales

A selection of our properties have plants for sale, from annuals sold from the greenhouse to fully stocked plant centres. We make sure that we have a range of varieties available to suit everyone – from the gardening amateur to the plant connoisseur. Why not try one of our exclusive varieties, such as *Primula* 'Inverewe', or one of our Trust-grown plants. We also stock a range of plants, bulbs and seeds all chosen by our experienced gardeners to reflect the properties' collections and the choicest blooms of the season.

For more information contact our properties or visit www.nts.org.uk

Please remember that all the proceeds from our plant centres go towards the upkeep of our properties.

AUTHENTIC GARDENING

Essential information before you visit

Photography and filming
The Trust welcomes photography for personal purposes in the grounds of all its properties, but for reasons of conservation and security, we regret that we cannot allow photography or filming inside our historic buildings. Images for lectures and commercial photography may be obtained from our Photo Librarian, tel 0844 493 2479.

Last minute
Please allow time for a relaxing and enjoyable visit. Generally it will not be possible to tour a property half an hour, or in some cases an hour, before closing time.

Group travel
The National Trust for Scotland welcomes all types of groups to its properties, no matter how big or small, and whether they are interested in a general Scottish experience or something very special, such as art, embroidery, architecture, archaeology, masonry, gardens and much more.

With its wide spectrum of properties, including splendid castles, impressive mansion houses, inspiring gardens, iconic battlefields, industrial heritage and town houses, as well as a glimpse of the life of Scots throughout the centuries, the Trust can provide you and your fellow travellers with a true Scottish experience.

Our itinerary suggestions will help you find the right tour for your group and the travel trade team will assist in making it happen. Further information is available at www.nts.org.uk/TravelTrade.

Guided tours ➜
At some of our busier or more fragile properties, visits are by regular timed guided tours. This enables you to have better viewing conditions and minimises wear and tear on historic interiors. You can also arrange a special guided tour if you call and book in advance. Our guides will be able to give you a unique insight into the properties and the lives of the people who lived there.

Please note that parts or all of some properties may be closed during normal opening hours due to functions.

Certain special event charges apply to Trust members too. Please contact the property before you visit.

After each property entry the days marked in **BOLD** show when a property is open.

All opening times are correct at time of going to print, but we would recommend checking the website or phoning in advance of making your journey.

Website

Have you visited the Trust's website yet? Whether you're planning a visit to one of our properties, looking for holiday accommodation or searching for an event nearby, you'll find inspiration at www.nts.org.uk. If using a smartphone, our website is mobile friendly, allowing quick and easy access to property details, directions and more.

Be sure to sign up for the Trust's e-newsletter to receive the latest news and receive exclusive offers and competitions. You can also join the conversation by following @N_T_S on Twitter, liking the National Trust for Scotland on Facebook or connecting with us on Kiltr.

Each property entry includes the OS grid reference, an indication of its location and how to get there.

Cycle

For cyclists, the nearest National Cycle Network (NCN) routes are given, eg NCN 75. For further information on the National Cycle Network contact Sustrans, tel (0845) 113 0065; website www.sustrans.co.uk

Bus

Bus information is shown where possible, and is correct at the time of going to press. Visitors are advised that many buses stop only at the entrance gates to castles or large properties. From there, a walk through the grounds of up to a mile may be necessary to reach the property itself.

Rail

The name of the nearest rail/underground station is shown where applicable, including the distance from the property. Information on tickets, train times and routes is available from: National Rail Enquiries, tel (08457) 484950; website www.nationalrail.co.uk or www.thetrainline.com

For all public transport information, contact Traveline Scotland, tel (0871) 200 2233; website www.travelinescotland.com

Ferry

Excellent ferry services exist to carry visitors to most Scottish islands. The major ferry company operating in the Hebrides and the Clyde is Caledonian MacBrayne. Smaller operators run daily, weekly or charter cruises to many

of the smaller islands. Sailings to Staffa are operated from Iona, Ulva and Fionnphort, and there are inclusive day tours to Staffa, Iona and Mull from Oban.

Details about services may be obtained from Tourist Information Centres and the sources listed below:

Most islands in the Firth of Clyde & Western Isles

Caledonian MacBrayne, Ferry Terminal, Gourock PA19 1QP. Tel 0800 066 5000; website www.calmac.co.uk

Canna, Rum, Eigg & Muck

Arisaig Marine (private charter), tel (01687) 450224; website www.arisaig.co.uk

Bruce Watt Cruises (private charter), Mallaig Harbour, tel (01687) 462320; website www.knoydart-ferry.co.uk

Staffa & Iona

Caledonian MacBrayne, in conjunction with local operators, run day tours from Oban in the summer.

Gordon Grant Tours, Achavaich, Iona. Tel (01681) 700 338; website www.staffatours.com

C Kirkpatrick, Tigh Na Traigh, Iona. Tel (01681) 700 358; website www.staffatrips.co.uk

Iain Morrison, Turus Mara, Penmore Mill, Dervaig, Mull. Freephone (08000) 858786; website www.turusmara.com

Bowman's Tours, tel (01631) 566809 or (01631) 563221; website www.bowmanstours.co.uk. (They provide a link between the ferry terminals on Mull at Craignure and Fionnphort.)

Loch Lomond

Sweeney's Cruises, tel (01389) 752376; website www.sweeneyscruises.com

Macfarlane's Mail Boat Cruises, tel (01360) 870214; website www.balmahaboatyard.co.uk

Orkney & Shetland

Northlink Ferries, tel (0845) 6000 449; website www.northlinkferries.co.uk

Pentland Ferries, tel (08156) 831226; website www.pentlandferries.co.uk

Orkney Ferries, tel (01856) 872044; website www.orkneyferries.co.uk

Dumfries & Galloway

Ardrossan
Innerleithen
Tarbolton
Ayr
Maybole
Kirkoswald
Grey Mare's Tail
Moffat
Dumfries
Thomas Carlyle's Birthplace
Castle Douglas
Ecclefechan
Carlisle
Threave Estate
Kirkcudbright
Rockcliffe
Broughton House

Broughton House & Garden

12 High Street, Kirkcudbright, Dumfries & Galloway DG6 4JX

tel/fax 0844 493 2246

Cross the threshold of Broughton House and enter the world of well-known Scottish artist E A Hornel, one of the 'Glasgow Boys'. Open to the public since April 2005 after a period of conservation, this fine 18th-century town house was bought by Hornel in 1901 and became his home and studio. Today, you can admire his paintings and those of his fellow artists throughout the house and gallery. Some of his extensive collection of books are on display in the library, including works by Burns and many books on local history. From the studio follow your gaze out into the enchanting garden, where you too may find inspiration in the light falling across the Dee.

E → 🏛 🎎 🎦 £ D

⊠ **OS Ref:** NX681511
Road: Off A711/A755
Cycle: NCN 7 **Bus:** McEwan's (Nos 500/X75, 501), Dumfries (28m) and Castle Douglas (9m) to Kirkcudbright

👶 Baby changing facilities, children's activities

❗ Two interactive computer touch screens available

💍 Civil wedding licence, exclusive dinners, private parties and receptions

🖵 Information sheets: French, German

♿ Entrance and toilet at lower ground level. Lift to upper ground floor. Part of garden can be viewed from studio

◈ Large print information

P Parking in street and in nearby car park in town centre

A The E A Hornel Trustees transferred ownership of the house to the Trust in 1997

Garden only	1 Feb to 22 Mar	11-4		**M T W T F . .**	
House and Garden	23 Mar to 31 Oct	12-5 (last entry 4.30)		**M T W T F S S**	

Thomas Carlyle's Birthplace

The Arched House, Ecclefechan, Lockerbie, Dumfries & Galloway DG11 3DG

tel 0844 493 2247

Looking upon this humble house today, it's inspiring to reflect that this was the birthplace of one of Britain's most influential thinkers. The great social historian Thomas Carlyle was born in 1795 in this house constructed by his father and uncle, both local stonemasons.

Carlyle left Ecclefechan at the age of 13 and walked the 84 miles to Edinburgh in order to attend university. This was just one of many remarkable achievements, as he went on to establish himself as one of the 19th century's leading voices on morals and social equality. You can find out more about Carlyle's life and work through the fascinating collection of portraits and personal belongings.

£ E

⊠ **OS Ref:** NY193745
Road: Off M74, on A74, in Ecclefechan, 5½m SE of Lockerbie, 6m NW of Gretna Green
Cycle: NCN 74 **Bus:** White Star and Stagecoach, Lockerbie to Ecclefechan
Rail: Lockerbie station, 5½m

→ Max 15 people

🏠 One step into building, several inside. One room downstairs, two rooms upstairs

◈ Large print information on request

P On road, within 50m of property

A Given in 1936 by the Trustees of Carlyle's House Memorial Fund

House	29 Mar to 1 Apr	12-4		**M . . . F S S**
	1 Jun to 30 Sep	12-4		**M . . . F S S**

Grey Mare's Tail Nature Reserve

Moffat Water Valley, Dumfries & Galloway DG10 9DP

tel 0844 493 2249

On a visit to Loch Skeen, Sir Walter Scott was thrown from his horse into a peat bog. Despite this unfortunate introduction, he was so inspired by the landscape that he later described the scene in his poem *Marmion*. The chances are that you'll be equally taken with this dramatic upland property, unfolding from the waterfall cascading into the Moffat Water Valley up steep slopes to Loch Skeen and the peak of White Coomb (821m) beyond.

The area is a paradise for botanists and wildlife enthusiasts, who come to observe the rare upland plants, peregrines and ring ouzels, feral goats and, occasionally, mountain hares. Historians, too, can seek out evidence of Iron Age settlers and 17th-century Covenanters who also took refuge here.

🚶 🅿 £ F

OS Ref: NT186144
Road: On A708, 10m NE of Moffat

Due to the challenging nature of the terrain, please heed all warning notices

Live CCTV link from June-July to the peregrine falcon nest in Tail Burn gorge. Dog walkers please be aware of livestock. No toilets at property

Waterfall viewpoint 60 metres from car park. Surrounding terrain difficult

Land extending to Loch Skeen and White Coomb (870ha) purchased in 1962 by the Trust's Mountainous Country Fund, formed by Percy Unna. Land at Dob's Linn (52ha) purchased in 1972

Nature Reserve   All year   **M T W T F S S**

Rockcliffe

Dumfries & Galloway

tel 0844 493 2244

Rockcliffe is one of Scotland's prettiest stretches of coastline. A network of paths gives access to most of the area, including the important Dark Age trading post of Mote of Mark. Broadleaved woodland, wildflower meadows and heather-topped rocky outcrops provide a range of wildlife habitats. Spring offers a stunning display of bluebells, with warblers and other birds arriving to breed. In summer, a diversity of butterflies

brings colour to the meadows. As the autumn colours appear, the swallows depart and wildfowl numbers begin to build. And the harsh winter months see large numbers of ducks and waders congregating in Rough Firth.

Rough Island is a 8ha (20a) bird sanctuary with nesting oystercatchers and ringed plovers. To prevent disturbance, please don't visit the island during May and June.

E 🚶 ⬦ 🏛 🅿

OS Ref: NX844540
Road: Off A710, 7m S of Dalbeattie
Bus: Regular service between Dalbeattie and Dumfries

Toilet at Rockcliffe. Part of Jubilee Path accessible

Mote of Mark and Rough Island (15ha) given in 1937 by John and James McLellan in memory of their brother, Col W McLellan, CBE. Muckle Lands and Jubilee Path (20ha) given in 1965 by Hilda G Longworth. Auchenvhin and Port Donnel bequeathed in 1969 with an endowment by Major J I A McDiarmid. Further areas of coastline presented by Mrs McLellan (1971) and Mrs Pimm (1990)

Rockcliffe   All year   **M T W T F S S**

Threave Estate

There's something to please everyone at Threave. Magnificent gardens and beautifully restored interiors. Wildlife and walks around the estate. Stop for a moment and listen to the trees…

Threave Estate

Castle Douglas, Dumfries & Galloway DG7 1RX

tel 0844 493 2245
fax 0844 493 2243

ranger/naturalist
tel 0844 493 2244

Threave's spectacular gardens have been created over the years by students of the Trust's School of Heritage Gardening. The gardens are constantly evolving to suit the needs of the school but they're open all year giving interest in every season. In spring, however, the gardens are carpeted with over 200 varieties of daffodil complementing the spring-flowering shrubs and trees. Later, you can admire succulent fruit and vegetables in the walled garden and glasshouses. And if that whets your appetite, there's also a well-stocked restaurant with delicious home-baking. Elsewhere you can enjoy the rock garden, rose garden, heathers, conifers and herbaceous perennials. Don't miss the various water features and recent additions to the garden – such as the sculpture garden, located in the formal garden, and the new bat trail which runs right through the garden. Lots of new plantings continue to add to Threave's extensive collection of plants.

After a turn around the gardens, enter the grand Scottish Baronial house, now fully restored to the way it was in the 1930s. Here you can join one of our guides and learn all about daily life for the Gordon family, who built the house in 1872, and for the household staff. Children, however, might be more interested in locating the secret drawer filled with sweets!

Visit the Countryside Centre to find out more about the estate's wildlife and conservation work before setting off to explore, perhaps to Threave Castle or by taking our new circular estate walk to the bird hides and osprey viewing platform overlooking the River Dee and Blackpark Marsh. This is a Special Protection Area for breeding waders and wintering wildfowl – pink-footed geese and Greenland white-fronted geese, now a globally threatened species, are regular visitors to the estate. And in summer you may be lucky enough to see otters and osprey fishing in the river.

OS Ref: NX753604
Road: Off A75, 1m W of Castle Douglas **Cycle:** NCN 7 **Bus:** McEwan's (No 501), Dumfries to Castle Douglas **Foot:** 1½m walk from Castle Douglas

Guided tours of house only, max 12 people. Two per hour, admission by timed ticket

Licensed restaurant plus outside terrace

Baby changing facilities, children's activities and quizzes

Only assistance dogs are allowed in the garden. Dogs are welcome on the estate and on the car park and drive side of the Visitor Centre

Civil wedding licence, exclusive dinners, private parties, receptions and marquee areas

Explanatory text: French, German, Italian, Spanish

Garden: hard paths, some inclines. Manual wheelchair and scooter (book in advance). Garden viewpoint. House: five rooms accessible, with lift to 1st floor. Visitor Centre, shop, restaurant, toilets

Guided touch tours of house (book in advance)

House and estate (492ha) given in 1948 by Major A F Gordon, DSO, MC, with a generous endowment. A further 113ha purchased in 1950 and 1959

Estate and Garden	All year		M	T	W	T	F	S	S
Visitor &	1 Feb to 22 Mar	10-5	.	.	.	.	F	S	S
Countryside Centres,	23 Mar to 31 Oct	10-5	M	T	W	T	F	S	S
Restaurant,									
Gift Shop, Plant Centre	1 Nov to 23 Dec	10-5	.	.	.	.	F	S	S
and Glasshouses									
House	23 Mar to 31 Oct	11-3.30	.	.	W	T	F	.	S

Visit to house by guided tour only and visitors are advised to book in advance.

Scottish Borders

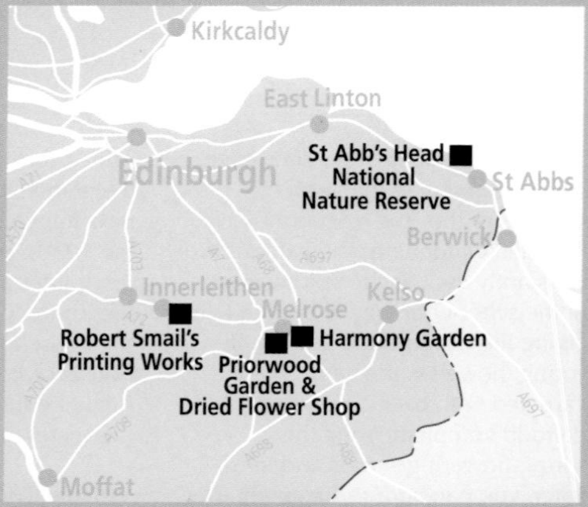

St Abb's Head ■
National
Nature Reserve

St Abbs

Kirkcaldy

East Linton

Edinburgh

Berwick

Innerleithen

Melrose

Kelso

Robert Smail's
Printing Works ■

■ Harmony Garden

Priorwood
Garden &
Dried Flower Shop ■

Moffat

web www.nts.org.uk

Harmony Garden

St Mary's Road, Melrose, Borders TD6 9LJ

tel 0844 493 2251

The name says it all. Surrounded by walls and screened by trees, the garden at Harmony offers a unique sense of peace and tranquillity. Stroll across the lush green lawns and admire the herbaceous and mixed borders, the vegetable and fruit areas, and, in spring, the rich display of bulbs.

Take a deep breath and survey the magnificent views across to Melrose Abbey and the Eildon Hills. If you simply can't tear yourself away from this idyllic setting, it's worth noting that the beautiful 19th-century house can now be hired for holidays or special occasions.

OS Ref: NT547342
Road: Off A6091, in Melrose, opposite the Abbey **Cycle:** NCN 1 **Bus:** First Edinburgh from Edinburgh and Peebles; (0871) 200 2233, plus other local bus companies

Book in advance

Parking at entrance. Much of garden accessible: gravel paths, some steps but may use grass area instead

Pay & Display 200 metres

D. Joint ticket with Priorwood Garden & Dried Flower Shop

Bequeathed in 1996 by Mrs Christian Pitman

Garden 23 Mar to 31 Oct 10-5 (Sun 1-5) **M T W T F S S**

Priorwood Garden & Dried Flower Shop

Melrose, Borders TD6 9PX

tel 0844 493 2257
shop tel 0844 493 2258

Priorwood is a specialist centre for the craft of dried flower arranging. Most of the flowers are grown for this purpose and the colourful selection brings variety to the arrangements made here. But you can simply enjoy the blossoms, especially in spring, or pause for a summer picnic within sight of the ruins of Melrose Abbey.

The garden also includes an orchard where you can see historic apple varieties being grown organically. From Priorwood it's a only a short walk to Harmony Garden (see above).

OS Ref: NT548341
Road: A68 Jedburgh Road, signposted for Melrose. Off A6091, in Melrose, adjacent to Abbey **Cycle:** NCN 1 **Bus:** First Edinburgh from Edinburgh and Peebles; (0871) 200 2233

Book in advance

Limited parking available at entrance. Ramp to shops and garden, gravel paths

Pay & Display 50 metres

D. Joint ticket with Harmony Garden

Purchased in 1974

Gift Shop	5 Jan to 22 Mar	12-4	**M T W T F S .**
	23 Mar to 31 Oct	10-5 (Sun 1-5)	**M T W T F S S**
	1 Nov to 24 Dec	10-4	**M T W T F S .**
Garden	23 Mar to 31 Oct	10-5 (Sun 1-5)	**M T W T F S S**
	1 Nov to 24 Dec	10-4	**M T W T F S .**

< St Abb's Head

Robert Smail's Printing Works

7/9 High Street, Innerleithen, Borders EH44 6HA

tel 0844 493 2259

Step back in time to a fully restored jobbing letterpress printers. Nothing was ever thrown away and you can still see the original office, full of records from 120 years of the business.

You'll see the water-wheel – the source of power until the 1930s. In the caseroom, our compositor will encourage you to have a go at typesetting – but you must mind your 'p's and 'q's! And our printer will demonstrate the original presses, which are still used today to print jobs such as business cards and wedding stationery.

Altogether, Smail's has something for everyone, with plenty of interaction and activities in an authentic setting.

E **£** D

OS Ref: NT332367
Road: 30m S of Edinburgh, A72, 6m from Peebles (Innerleithen Road)
Cycle: NCN 1 **Bus:** First Edinburgh from Edinburgh or Peebles; (0871) 200 2233

Allow at least 1 hour

Includes a wide range of letterpress products printed on the premises. Shop also open in run-up to Christmas

Children's activities and quizzes, baby backpacks allowed, storage for pushchairs

No toilet on premises. Coach parties welcome, pre-booking necessary

Drop-off point at front door. Shop, office, paper store and machine room accessible. Stairs to composing room

Outside property, car park 5 mins' walk

Purchased from Cowan Smail in 1986

			M			T	F	S	S
Printing Works	23 Mar to 31 Oct	12-5 (Sun 1-5)	**M**			**T**	**F**	**S**	**S**
Shop	23 Mar to 31 Oct	12-5 (Sun 1-5)	**M**			**T**	**F**	**S**	**S**
	8 Nov to 23 Dec	10-4 (Sat 9-3)	**M**			**T**	**F**	**S**	

St Abb's Head National Nature Reserve

Ranger's Cottage, Northfield, St Abbs, Eyemouth, Borders TD14 5QF

tel/fax 0844 493 2256

St Abb's Head has spectacular cliff-top scenery and a chance to feel as if you are somewhere really wild just a short walk from civilisation. In the summer months tens of thousands of nesting seabirds jostle for space on the cliffs and beautiful carpets of wildflowers adorn the grasslands behind. The Reserve boasts a wealth of other wildlife, as do the surrounding inshore waters, which form part of Scotland's only Voluntary Marine Reserve. You can learn more about the wildlife and history of the area, both above and below the waves, at the Nature Centre, or join a ranger-led walk along the cliff tops or on the shore.

OS Ref: NT912692
Road: Off A1107, 2m N of Coldingham

(not National Trust for Scotland)

Parking. Toilet. Nature Reserve Centre accessible, possibly with assistance. Access by car to lighthouse viewpoint

Please use car park beside Nature Reserve Centre at Northfield Farm steading: the lighthouse car park is reserved for people with walking difficulties

Land at St Abb's Head (76ha) purchased in 1980. Lumsdaine coastal strip (68ha) donated by Pearl Assurance Company Ltd in 1984. Blackpotts grazings (50ha) purchased in 1994

			M	T	W	T	F	S	S
Nature Reserve	All year		**M**	**T**	**W**	**T**	**F**	**S**	**S**
Nature Centre	29 Mar to 31 Oct	10-5	**M**	**T**	**W**	**T**	**F**	**S**	**S**

Scotland's National Nature Reserves

Edinburgh & the Lothians

Edinburgh

The Georgian House

Gladstone's Land

Caiy Stane

Montrose

Forfar

St Andrews

Preston Mill & Phantassie Doocot

House of the Binns

Newhailes

Inveresk Lodge Garden

East Linton

St Abbs

Glasgow

Malleny Garden

Berwick

Innerleithen

Kelso

web www.nts.org.uk

The Georgian House
7 Charlotte Square, Edinburgh EH2 4DR

tel/fax 0844 493 2118 or
tel 0844 493 2117

Step back in time to the elegance and refinement of Edinburgh's New Town in the late 18th century – a time when Edinburgh's well-to-do left the cramped, squalid conditions of the Old Town to settle in the fashionable New Town. The Georgian House was built in 1796 for John Lamont, 18th Chief of the Clan Lamont, and he lived here with his family until 1815.

Imagine how it must have felt to be the first owner of this magnificent Robert Adam-designed town house – and to pay just £1,800 for the privilege! Explore John's home to discover what life was like for the wealthy in Edinburgh's New Town 200 years ago. Contrast this with the 'below stairs' life of the household staff who made this elegant lifestyle possible.

The Georgian House was restored in the early 1970s and over the past few years there has been an ongoing programme of redecoration to bring it back to its pristine 1975 condition. The exquisite collections of china, silver, paintings and furniture all reflect the domestic life and social and economic context of the times.

Don't miss our short film, *Living in a Grand Design*, which depicts life in Edinburgh's New Town. Find out more about New Town life from the touch screen computers in the basement – history at your fingertips!

Younger visitors can complete the Activity Guide or the Collection Trail using flashcards, and have fun in the activity room (dressing up in replica costumes or investigating the handling objects). There is also a Wee Guide available for purchase.

On Saturday afternoons during July and August visitors can experience a flavour of 18th-century life with guides in costume in some of the display rooms. Costumed, scripted tours of the house take place in November each year – please phone or email for details.

At the end of your visit don't miss the gift shop, which has a wide range of merchandise catering for all tastes.

E   ☐   £ D

Road: Edinburgh city centre, 2 mins from west end of Princes Street **Cycle:** NCN 1, 75 **Tour buses:** From Waverley station **Bus:** Lothian Buses (Nos 37, 40, 41) to Charlotte Square; (0131) 555 6363 **Rail:** 15 mins' walk from Waverley and Haymarket stations

For groups, by prior arrangement

Storage for two pushchairs, baby changing facilities, children's activities in school holidays, children's activity guide

Civil wedding licence, receptions

Touch-screen CD-Rom, audio-visual presentation

Explanatory text: Arabic, Chinese, Danish, Dutch, French, German, Hungarian, Italian, Japanese, Polish, Portuguese, Russian, Spanish, Swedish

Six steps to front door, stairs inside house. On-street parking, portable chairs available, 'armchair' guide and portable DVD player to view film

Braille guidebook. Large print information. Guided touch tour (book in advance)

Subtitled video with induction loop

Metered spaces in Charlotte Square

Nos 5-7 conveyed to the Trust through National Land Fund procedures in 1966

House										
	1 Mar to 24 Mar	11-4	M	T	W	T	F	S	S
	25 Mar to 30 Jun	10-5	M	T	W	T	F	S	S
	1 Jul to 31 Aug	10-6	M	T	W	T	F	S	S
	1 Sep to 31 Oct	10-5	M	T	W	T	F	S	S
	1 Nov to 30 Nov	11-3	M	T	W	T	F	S	S

Last admission 30 mins before closing.

Gladstone's Land

477B Lawnmarket, Edinburgh EH1 2NT

tel 0844 493 2120
fax 0844 493 2119

Step back in time to bustling and turbulent 17th-century Edinburgh. Thomas Gledstanes, a wealthy merchant who owned this six-storey tenement, rented each floor to tenants of various means. Explore Thomas's land to discover the lives of his tenants and experience what life was really like in Edinburgh's Old Town 400 years ago.

From the windows, occupants over the years would have observed many important events in Scottish history – Charles I en route to his coronation at Holyrood Palace in 1633, the arrival of Bonnie Prince Charlie in 1745, and the visit of George IV in 1822.

View six display rooms furnished with objects of the period, and including an original painted ceiling dating to 1620. Discover the differences between 17th- and 18th-century living standards in the Green Room – a Georgian extension, which includes an original Norie painted panel.

On Saturday afternoons during July and August visitors can experience a flavour of 17th-century life, when there are guides in costume in the display rooms.

Younger visitors can enjoy taking part in the prize draw competition by completing a discovery trail. There are three discovery trails with varying degrees of difficulty to suit all ages. A follow-on activity booklet to be completed at home, the Wee Guide, is available for purchase in the gift shop.

The Gladstone Gallery, open daily (except Mondays) during July and August, is a free art gallery exhibiting local contemporary artwork and boasts another painted ceiling. Please see the website or call the property for up-to-date Gladstone Gallery listings.

At the end of your visit don't miss the gift shop, which has a vast array of merchandise catering for all tastes.

E ☐ ▦ £ D

Road: Lawnmarket, at top end of Royal Mile **Cycle:** 1m from NCN 1, 75 **Foot:** 5 mins' walk from Tourist Information Centre on Princes Street (near Waverley Station) via the Mound

Groups of 10 or more should book in advance

Children's discovery trails

Information sheets: Dutch, French, German, Italian, Japanese, Norwegian, Spanish, Russian, Polish, Swedish, Portuguese, Mandarin, Hungarian

No parking outside. Four steep steps from road to pavement outside property; pavement ramp 100 metres. Ground floor only, but 'armchair visits' offered

Braille guidebook. Large-print room information sheets

Purchased in 1934

House											
	23 Mar to 30 Jun	10-5	**M**	**T**	**W**	**T**	**F**	**S**	**S**		
	1 Jul to 31 Aug	10-6.30	**M**	**T**	**W**	**T**	**F**	**S**	**S**		
	1 Sep to 31 Oct	10-5	**M**	**T**	**W**	**T**	**F**	**S**	**S**		

Last admission 30 mins before closing.

House of the Binns

Linlithgow, West Lothian EH49 7NA

tel 0844 493 2127
ranger service
tel 0844 493 2124

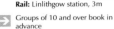

The House of the Binns stands as a living monument to one of Scotland's oldest families, the Dalyells, who have lived here since 1612. It contains a fascinating collection of 17th- to 20th-century furniture, porcelain and portraits revealing the family's lives and interests through the centuries. Military historians take note – it was here in 1681 that General Tam Dalyell formed the legendary regiment of Royal Scots Greys. Students of architecture, meanwhile, will be interested to see how the house reflects the 17th-century transition from fortified stronghold to spacious mansion. Leaving the house, a woodland walk, carpeted with snowdrops and daffodils in spring, takes you to a panoramic viewpoint over the Firth of Forth.

OS Ref: NT051785
Road: Off A904, 15m W of Edinburgh
Rail: Linlithgow station, 3m

Groups of 10 and over book in advance

Explanatory text: Chinese, Dutch, French, German, Japanese, Polish, Russian, Spanish

Parking at main door by arrangement. Ground floor accessible. 'Armchair visit' and photograph album of upper floors. Toilet

Braille information sheets. Guided tours

File of information on history of property

C. Members of the Royal Scots Dragoon Guards (successors of 'The Greys') in uniform are admitted free

House, with pictures, plenishings and policies (87ha), given in 1944 by the late Eleanor Dalyell and her son Tam Dalyell, with an endowment

			M T W T F S S
Estate	All year, gates closed at 7.30pm		M T W T F S S
House	1 Jun to 30 Sep	2-5	M T W . . S S

Guided tours only. Last tour of house at 4.15.

Inveresk Lodge Garden

24 Inveresk Village, Musselburgh, East Lothian EH21 7TE

tel 0844 493 2126
ranger service
tel 0844 493 2124

A must-visit destination for all keen gardeners, this delightful hillside garden is just awaiting discovery. Tucked away within its stone boundary walls you will find unusual plants as well as familiar friends growing within the mixed beds and borders. You'll also be drawn to the beautiful restored Victorian conservatory which is home to an aviary. The garden is a true treat for the senses with many scented plants and enchanting birdsong. Below the garden lies the meadow and pond, a haven for wildlife just waiting to be spotted.

OS Ref: NT348716
Road: A6124, S of Musselburgh, 6m E of Edinburgh **Cycle:** 1m from NCN 1
Bus: Lothian Buses from Edinburgh city centre; (0131) 555 6363

Pond dipping platform

Dogs are not allowed in the garden

Parking at entrance with four steps. Entrance 100 metres left of main entrance, assistance required to open it from garden side. Conservatory and some of garden accessible. Toilet

Scented plants

By garden wall

Presented by Helen E Brunton in 1959

			M T W T F S S
Garden	All year	10-5 or dusk if earlier	M T W T F S S

Malleny Garden

Balerno, Edinburgh EH14 7AF

tel 0844 493 2123

Much appreciated for its atmosphere of peace and tranquillity, Malleny is the garden to visit for a few hours of quiet contemplation among beautiful surroundings. Renowned for its flamboyant plantings of old-fashioned roses, and herbaceous perennials arranged with an eye for pleasing colour combinations, this 1.2ha (3a) walled garden is dominated by four magnificent clipped yew trees dating from the 17th century. You can also enjoy the vegetable and herb garden, the Victorian greenhouse, and the surrounding area of woodland which adds to the aura of shelter and seclusion.

The doocot, adjacent to the privately let house, has been repaired with financial assistance from Historic Scotland. Access can be arranged by contacting the Property Manager.

E ▮ **P** **£**ᴱ

OS Ref: NT165665
Road: Off Lanark Road (A70)
Cycle: 1m from NCN 75 **Bus:** Lothian Buses (No 44) from Edinburgh city centre; (0131) 555 6363, or First Edinburgh (Nos 44/66); (0871) 200 2233 **Rail:** Curriehill station (on Glasgow to Edinburgh line)

Only assistance dogs are allowed in the garden

Drop-off point at small gate by Malleny House. Garden: gravel paths, so assistance required

Scented plants

A House and garden (9a) presented to the Trust with an endowment by the late Mrs Gore-Browne Henderson in 1968

| Garden | All year | 10-5 or dusk if earlier | **M T W T F S S** |

Preston Mill & Phantassie Doocot

East Linton, East Lothian EH40 3DS

tel 0844 493 2128
ranger service
tel 0844 493 2124

With its distinctive conical-roofed kiln and red pantiled buildings, it's no wonder Preston Mill is so popular with artists and photographers. The nearby millpond completes the idyllic rural scene. There's been a mill on this site since the 16th century and the present stone buildings date from the 18th century. The water-wheel and the grain milling machinery it powers are relatively modern and the mill remained in operation until 1959. You can see and hear the mechanisms in action and learn about the history of Preston Mill and the millers who worked there. After a picnic lunch, wander past the millpond to the unusual doocot, once home to 500 birds.

Exhibition and interpretation, interactive displays and Explorer Packs – great for families. See website for special events.

E ▮ ▮ ▮ **P**
£ᴰ

OS Ref: NT596779
Road: Off A1, in East Linton, 23m east of Edinburgh **Bus:** First Edinburgh, Edinburgh to East Linton; (0871) 200 2233

Access to mill building by guided tour, which run approx every 45 mins. Booking essential for groups of 10 or more or to avoid disappointment

Drinks and snacks

Baby changing facilities, baby backpacks not allowed, storage for pushchairs, children's activities

Explanatory text: Dutch, French, German, Italian, Japanese, Spanish

Drop-off point in front of Mill. Car park nearby. Ground floor, exhibition room, shop, toilet. Photograph album available to view

A Preston Mill given in 1950 by the Trustees of John Gray. Phantassie Doocot given in 1962 by Mr W Hamilton

| Mill & Doocot | 2 May to 30 Sep | 12.30-5 | **M . . T F S S** |

Newhailes

Newhailes Road, Musselburgh, East Lothian EH21 6RY

tel 0844 493 2125
ranger service
tel 0844 493 2124

Newhailes is an amazing survival story. This means you can experience this dignified 17th-century home and its 18th-century additions in authentic condition. With much of the original decorative scheme – the Chinese hand-painted wallpaper, painted woodwork and furnishings – surviving intact, the interiors have mellowed beautifully, adding greatly to the character of the house. Newhailes is also a unique achievement in conservation terms. Rather than attempt to re-create an immaculate dwelling, the Trust has worked hard to keep the house 'untouched' by modern hands.

If you're hungry for Scottish history, Newhailes features prominently in the Scottish Enlightenment. Sir David Dalrymple, one of Newhailes' most illustrious owners, built the library in 1718. Unusual because of its size and prominent placement, it was probably the largest private library of its time in Scotland.

It's easy to imagine key figures of the Enlightenment gathered in this room for discussion and debate surrounded by Dalrymple's vast collection of books (currently held in the care of the National Library of Scotland). Dr Johnson himself reportedly described the library as 'the most learned drawing room in Europe'.

The 18th-century designed landscape surrounding the house holds a few surprises of its own. Take time to explore and you will discover a raised walkway, a shell grotto hidden in the trees and a water garden, as well as a number of different walks and paths. Research continues to reveal the original layout of the landscape, with new interpretation and map for 2013. Please also see website for a variety of property and ranger-led events throughout the year, or ask at the Visitor Centre. New Enlightenment exhibition in the Education Room from May 2013.

OS Ref: NT327725
Road: In Musselburgh on the Newhailes Road (A6095)
Cycle: NCN1 runs nearby. Good cycle paths from Edinburgh city centre **Bus:** Lothian Buses No 30 (from front gate) and Nos 26/44 (from north gate through estate) from Edinburgh city centre; (0131) 555 6363, First Edinburgh (Nos 140/141); (0871) 200 2233 **Rail:** Musselburgh or Newcraighall stations, 20 mins' walk

(not National Trust for Scotland)

All access to house by guided tour only

Stables café. Dogs on lead in courtyard

Baby changing facilities, baby backpacks not allowed in house, storage for pushchairs, monthly children's club (contact Ranger Service for details)

Explanatory text: Dutch, French, German, Italian

Drop-off point at Visitor Centre and in front of house. Visitor Centre: shop, café, interpretation, toilets. House: basement entrance with lift to principal floor. Photograph album and information of two rooms on upper floor. All-ability path in part of water garden woods

Large print copy of audio-visual script

Induction loop for main audio-visual presentation. Hearing loop system available on request

House and policies donated by the Trustees of Sir C M Dalrymple. Contents acquired in 1997 with assistance from the Heritage Lottery Fund and the National Art Collections Fund

				M T W T F S S
Estate	All year	dawn to dusk		**M T W T F S S**
House	29 Mar to 1 Apr	12-5		**M** . . . **F S S**
	2 May to 30 Sep	12-5		**M** . . **T F S S**
Visitor Centre,	29 Mar to 1 Apr	11-5		**M** . . . **F S S**
Shop and Café	6 Apr to 29 Apr	11-4		**M** . . . . **S S**
	2 May to 30 Sep	11-5		**M** . . **T F S S**
	1 Oct to 31 Oct	11-4		. . . . . **S S**

Guided tours only. Tours last approx 1¼ hours, starting every 30 mins from Visitor Centre. First tour departs 12.00; last tour departs 3.30pm. Please allow 15 mins prior to your departure to collect tickets and view introductory film.
Reservation line: 0844 493 2125. *Reservations advised to avoid disappointment.*

Fife

web www.nts.org.uk

Pitlochry
Montrose
Forfar
Glamis
Dunkeld
Dundee
Perth
Hill of Tarvit Mansionhouse & Garden
St Andrews
Falkland Palace & Garden
Kellie Castle & Garden
Stirling
Kirkcaldy
Royal Burgh of Culross
Edinburgh
East Linton

Royal Burgh of Culross

Culross, Fife KY12 8JH

tel 0844 493 2189
fax 0844 493 2190

Culross is a living, breathing open-air museum. Wander the historic streets of this once-thriving port on the River Forth, a hive of industry in the 17th century thanks to coal mining, salt panning and the now obsolete trade of iron girdle making. Get a sense of what it would have been like to live in Culross Palace in its prime, with original painted woodwork and beautifully restored 17th and 18th-century interiors. Upstairs in the attic rooms there is a fascinating and informative exhibition on witchcraft and also herbal remedies.

Take a guided tour of the town, Study and Town House, leaving from the palace reception every hour. Upstairs in the Town House there are elegant Georgian interiors and downstairs is a spooky cell. The Study, where Bishop Leighton of Dunblane reputedly composed his sermons, has stunning views across the Forth.

The delightful palace garden is full of herbs, fruit and vegetables (which you can buy in season), just as it would have been during its heyday. Grab an information card and see how many of our large collection of period plants you can identify and learn how they were used. The view from the top terrace is spectacular.

Afterwards, explore the rest of the town, taking in evocatively named places such as Stinking Wynd, as well as the ruins of St Mungo's Chapel, the abbey, the old monastery and the West Kirk. See the many beautifully preserved small houses within the Outstanding Conservation Area, and don't miss Culross Harbour, which is believed to be one of the oldest in Scotland, first used by the monks of Culross Abbey.

After all this exploration, reward yourself with a refreshing cup of tea and one of the famous scones from Bessie's Tearoom, and visit our shop which has a fine selection of gifts.

OS Ref: NS985859
Road: Off A985, 12m W of Forth Road Bridge, 4m E of Kincardine Bridge, 6m W of Dunfermline, 15m W of Edinburgh city centre **Cycle:** 3m from NCN 76 **Bus:** Stagecoach, Stirling to Dunfermline; (01383) 621249. First Edinburgh to Dunfermline; (0871) 200 2233 **Rail:** Falkirk station, 12m; Dunfermline station, 6m

→ £30 per guide, max 20 people

Tearoom

Baby changing facilities, storage for pushchairs, children's quizzes

Dogs can be left by reception whilst owners visit the Palace

Wedding ceremonies, private parties and receptions

Guidebook: French, German. Explanatory text: Catalan, Dutch, French, German, Hebrew, Italian, Japanese, Spanish

Cobbled streets. Drop-off points: Palace, Town House, Study. Bessie Bar tearoom with toilet. Slide viewer of internal/external Trust properties and village houses

Stairs to Palace, Town House, Study

Braille and large print guide: Palace, Town House, Study

Subtitled video on history of Culross

P Coaches in East car park, cars in West car park, 200 metres from Palace

A Palace purchased in 1932. St Mungo's Chapel presented by the Earl of Elgin (1947). Town House and The Study presented by the Royal Burgh (1975)

Garden	All year	10-6 or dusk if earlier	M	T	W	T	F	S	S
Palace, Study, Town House and Bessie's Tearoom*	23 Mar to 31 May	12-5	M	.	.	T	F	S	S
	1 Jun to 30 Aug	12-5	M	T	W	T	F	S	S
	1 Sep to 30 Sep	12-5	M	.	.	T	F	S	S
	1 Oct to 31 Oct	12-4	M	.	.	.	F	S	S

* Tearoom closes 30 mins later

Access to the Study and Town House is by guided tour only. Tours depart from palace reception every hour. First tour departs 1pm, last tour departs 4pm (3pm in October). Tours last approx 1 hour. Last entry to palace 45 mins before closing. Visits outside these times for pre-booked groups by arrangement with property.

Falkland Palace & Garden

A stunning 16th-century Renaissance palace set in the gentle scenery of Fife, this was the royal hunting palace and country retreat of the Stuart kings and queens. It's also home to Britain's oldest royal or real tennis court.

Falkland Palace & Garden

Falkland, Cupar, Fife KY15 7BU

tel 0844 493 2186
fax 0844 493 2188
shop tel 0844 493 2187

Wandering around the palace and gardens at Falkland, it's poignant to reflect that Mary, Queen of Scots spent some of the happiest days of her life here, 'playing the country girl in the woods and parks'.

The magnificent Royal Palace of Falkland was built by James IV and James V between 1500 and 1541 as their country residence. The Stuarts used Falkland as a lodge when hunting deer and wild boar in the forests of Fife. Portraits of the Stuart kings and queens hang in the palace and you can get a flavour of palace life when you enter the King's Bedchamber and the Queen's Room, both restored by the Trust. The Chapel Royal and the Keeper's Apartments in the Gatehouse are also on view to visitors.

Garden enthusiasts will appreciate the work of Percy Cane, who designed the gardens between 1947 and 1952 – this is the only known complete example of Cane's work left in Scotland. There are colourful herbaceous borders, lush green lawns and many unusual shrubs and trees, as well as a small herb garden featuring quotations from John Gerard's book *Herbal* (1597).

A world away from Wimbledon is the Royal Tennis Court, built in 1539. This is Britain's oldest tennis court, which today is home to a flourishing local royal tennis club. You can learn more about this fascinating corner of history from the dedicated exhibition.

Contact the palace or visit our website for details of events held throughout the year.

OS Ref: NO253075
Road: A912, 10m from M90, junction 8, 11m N of Kirkcaldy **Cycle:** NCN 1
Bus: Stagecoach Fife stops in High Street (100 metres); (01592) 610686

By prior arrangement, max 25 people

Baby changing facilities, Palace not suitable for pushchairs, storage for pushchairs, children's activity sheets

Only assistance dogs are allowed in garden. Large bags and rucksacks not allowed in palace

Civil wedding licence for palace gardens, marquee areas for exclusive dinners, private parties and receptions

Guidebook: French, German. Explanatory text: Dutch, French, German, Italian, Japanese, Spanish, Swedish. Audio tour: French, German, Italian, Spanish

Drop-off point near entrance. Palace not accessible, but 'armchair visit' available via audio wand and guidebook. Garden has gravel paths. Manual wheelchair available

Audio wand for Palace and garden. Scented garden

Inductive ear loop using 'T' switch

In Falkland village, c120 metres from the Palace

B. Scots Guards and members of Scots Guards Association get in free if wearing their badge or tie

Major Michael Crichton Stuart, MC, MA, Hereditary Constable and Keeper of Falkland Palace, appointed the Trust as Deputy Keeper in 1952 and provided an endowment for future upkeep. Falkland Town Hall purchased in 1986

Palace and Garden	1 Mar to 31 Oct	11-5 (Sun 1-5)	M T W T F S S
Shop	1 Mar to 31 Oct	11-5 (Sun 1-5)	M T W T F S S
	1 Nov to 23 Dec	11-4 (Sun 1-4)	M T W T F S S
	3 Jan to 28 Feb 2014	11-4 (Sun 1-4)	M T W T F S S

Last admission to palace 4.30.
Visits outside these times for pre-booked groups by arrangement with property.

Hill of Tarvit Mansionhouse & Garden

Cupar, Fife KY15 5PB

tel/fax 0844 493 2185

Nestling on a hillside in the Fife countryside, this early 20th-century family home is a gem. The house was remodelled in 1906 by the Scottish architect Sir Robert Lorimer (see Kellie Castle) around Mr F B Sharp's collection of French and Chippendale-style furniture, porcelain and paintings. Don't miss the kitchen premises for a fascinating insight into 'life below stairs'.

Lorimer also designed the gardens, with formal lawns, yew hedging, flowering borders and a sunken rose garden. The walled garden to the north contains sumptuous mixed borders and from here you can follow the paths to the hilltop viewpoint and the wider estate.

The grounds also contain a recently reinstated 9-hole hickory golf course, providing an innovative and memorable experience for all players. See www.kingarrock.com for more details.

£ C

OS Ref: NO378118
Road: Off A916, 2m S of Cupar
Cycle: 1m from NCN 1 **Bus:** Stagecoach Fife to Ceres, 1m; (01334) 474238
Rail: Cupar station, 2m

Out of hours opening for groups by prior arrangement

Tearoom

Pushchairs ground floor only, tearoom and shop. Baby backpacks not allowed. Children's activity sheets

Dog walkers please be aware of livestock

Civil wedding licence, exclusive dinners, private parties, receptions and marquee areas

Explanatory text: Dutch, French, German, Italian, Polish, Spanish, Japanese

Parking at house. Front door ramp to ground floor, shop, tearoom. Wheelchair available. Gravel paths in garden. Toilet

Bequeathed in 1949 by Miss E C Sharp with 503ha of gardens, forest and farmland. Present holding 198ha

				M	T	W	T	F	S	S
Garden and Grounds	All year	9.30-6 or dusk if earlier (garden)		M	T	W	T	F	S	S
House and Shop	23 Mar to 27 Oct	1-5		M	.	.	T	F	S	S
Tearoom (Hatters & Co)	23 Mar to 27 Oct	11-5		M	.	.	T	F	S	S

Last entry 4.15; tearoom subject to variation.
Visits outside these times for pre-booked parties by arrangement with property

Kellie Castle & Garden

Pittenweem, Fife KY10 2RF

tel 0844 493 2184
fax 0844 493 2183

Kellie Castle, completed around 1606 and once home to the Earls of Kellie, was restored by the Lorimer family in 1878. The oldest tower, dating back to 1360, is said to be haunted, but today the castle is a tranquil spot. Admire the magnificent plaster ceilings and panelling, and furniture designed by Sir Robert Lorimer. Visit the old stables, now housing an exhibition on Hew Lorimer's life, and see his sculpture studio. Take a stroll in the magical Arts & Crafts garden and enjoy the scent of old roses and the beautiful herbaceous borders growing harmoniously next to fruit and vegetables, all of which have been managed using organic methods for over 20 years.

£ C

OS Ref: NO520052
Road: On B9171, 3m NNW of Pittenweem **Bus:** Flexibus from local villages by pre-booking; (01334) 840340

By prior arrangement

Tearoom

Baby changing facilities, baby backpacks allowed, storage for pushchairs, adventure playground, children's quizzes

Explanatory text: French, German, Italian, Japanese, Spanish, Swedish, Chinese, Polish

Ground floor of castle. Shop, tearoom, toilets, garden. Wheelchair available

Audio guides, large print guides. Scented plants

Subtitled video of Hew Lorimer's work

Castle, garden and 6.5ha purchased in 1970. Main contents given to the Trust by the Secretary of State for Scotland. Lorimer family artefacts purchased in 1998

				M	T	W	T	F	S	S
Garden and Estate	All year	9.30-6 or dusk if earlier (garden)		M	T	W	T	F	S	S
Castle, Shop	23 Mar to 31 May	12.30-5**		M	T	W	.	.	S	S
and Tearoom*	1 Jun to 1 Sep	12.30-5		M	T	W	T	F	S	S
	4 Sep to 30 Oct	12.30-5 (4pm in Oct)		M	T	W	.	.	S	S

Tearoom open at 10.30, last orders at 4.30. Last entry to castle 45 mins before closing.
** *Open on Good Friday (29 Mar)*
Visits outside these times for pre-booked groups by arrangement with property.

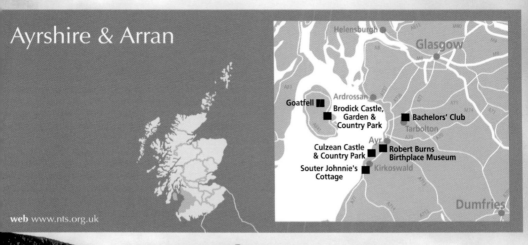

Ayrshire & Arran

Goatfell

Brodick Castle, Garden & Country Park

Bachelors' Club

Culzean Castle & Country Park

Robert Burns Birthplace Museum

Souter Johnnie's Cottage

Helensburgh

Glasgow

Ardrossan

Ayr

Tarbolton

Kirkoswald

Dumfries

web www.nts.org.uk

Brodick Castle, Garden & Country Park

A centuries-old castle and gardens set against the towering peak of Goatfell. Board the Arran ferry at Ardrossan on your way to Brodick and you'll find yourself embarking on a truly Scottish adventure.

Brodick Castle, Garden & Country Park

Isle of Arran KA27 8HY

tel 0844 493 2152
fax 0844 493 2153
ranger service
tel 0844 493 2154

Brodick Castle, its gardens and country park stretch from the shore to the highest peak on Arran. Crossing from the mainland, the journey alone is memorable with spectacular views of Goatfell from the ferry.

The castle, ancient seat of the Dukes of Hamilton, was the home of the Duke and Duchess of Montrose until 1957. Imagine what it must have been like to live in this fantastic location, surrounded by fine paintings, antique furniture and precious objects, all of which you can still see today. If you hear any mysterious sounds during your visit – don't be alarmed. It could be one of the many ghosts who've reputedly shared the castle with the owners over its 800-year history.

The woodland garden is worth a visit at any time of year, but comes into its own during spring when the famous collections of rhododendrons bloom. Why not join one of our garden guides for a walk around the walled garden, which dates from 1710 – a sheltered haven for tender plants from around the world.

Still in the mood for walking? Then venture out into the country park and discover wildflower meadows where Highland cows graze, woodland trails and tumbling waterfalls. Our trail guides can help you find hidden treasures such as the old carriageways and summerhouses of the Victorian age. And you can find out more about the park's wildlife at the Countryside Centre. There's also an exciting adventure playground for the kids to let off steam! Finally, after so much activity, stop to recharge your batteries at Brodick's coffee house or restaurant.

Families are made especially welcome in this lovely house, with a variety of self-guided activities available for our younger visitors. Throughout the season, dedicated staff also lead guided tours aimed specifically at children from 3 to 11 years of age. Occasionally adult tours take in parts of the castle not normally accessible to the public and, weather permitting, a visit to the battlements.

E · 🚶 · 🔖 · 🏠 · ❄ · ⛩
🏨 · P · £ B

OS Ref: NS015378
Cycle: NCN 73 **Ferry:** Ardrossan to Brodick (55 mins), connecting bus to Reception Centre (2m). Ferry between Claonaig (Kintyre) and Lochranza (north Arran), frequent in summer, limited in winter; tel Caledonian MacBrayne. All-inclusive travel and admission ticket from Strathclyde Passenger Transport stations; (0871) 200 2233

Tearoom, coffee house, with spaces outside in fine weather

Baby changing facilities, pushchairs ground floor only, buggies and slings available to use around castle, adventure playground, children's activities

Dogs on a lead are allowed in the woodland garden and Country Park

Civil wedding licence, marquee areas for exclusive dinners, private parties and receptions

Guidebook: French, German. Explanatory text: Chinese, Dutch, French, German, Italian, Japanese, Norwegian, Polish, Spanish, Swedish

Parking at castle and Reception Centre. Two wheelchairs available at castle, motorised wheelchair pre-bookable for grounds. Ground floor accessible: entrance hall, restaurant, toilets. Chairlift to old kitchen and silver room. Shop. Virtual tour and armchair photographic guide available. Electric bus from Reception Centre to castle. Wilma's Walk and top part of walled garden suitable

Main rooms on 1st floor up broad staircase

Braille information sheets in castle. Audio tours: castle and grounds

Inductive ear hook loop for audio tour of castle

Castle and 'associated chattels' accepted in lieu of estate duty by the Commissioners of Inland Revenue in 1958, and in turn accepted by the Trust at the request of the Treasury. The gardens and policies form a Country Park managed by the Trust on behalf of a joint committee representing North Ayrshire Council and the the National Trust for Scotland

			M	T	W	T	F	S	S
Country Park	All year	9.30-sunset	M	T	W	T	F	S	S
Castle	27 Mar to 30 Apr	11-3	M	T	W	T	F	S	S
	1 May to 30 Sep	11-4	M	T	W	T	F	S	S
	1 Oct to 31 Oct*	11-3	M	T	W	T	F	S	S
Shop and Tearoom	27 Mar to 30 Apr	10-4	M	T	W	T	F	S	S
	1 May to 31 Aug	10-5	M	T	W	T	F	S	S
	1 Sep to 30 Sep	10-4	M	T	W	T	F	S	S
	1 Oct to 31 Oct	11-4	M	T	W	T	F	S	S
Walled Garden	27 Mar to 31 Oct	10-4.30	M	T	W	T	F	S	S
	1 Nov to 20 Dec	10-3.30	·	·	·	·	·	S	S

Guided tours in October. Last admission to castle 30 mins before closing.

Goatfell

Isle of Arran

tel 0844 493 2155

Wild, open Goatfell, at 874m (2,866ft), is the highest peak on Arran. Walkers and mountaineers who venture into this dramatic and challenging upland landscape are rewarded with spectacular views of the island and, on a clear day, across to Ben Lomond, Jura and the coast of Ireland. Yet despite its rugged character, Goatfell is a fragile environment and we're working hard to preserve the heather, juniper trees and woodland areas that provide a vital habitat for mountain wildlife. Footpaths, too, have suffered from erosion and over the past 30 years the Trust has repaired many paths on Goatfell and around Glen Rosa. You're welcome to enjoy this wonderful landscape, but please stick to the paths and leave no trace of your visit.

OS Ref: NR991415
Cycle: Near NCN 73 **Foot:** Access from Brodick Country Park and Cladach on the A841, Brodick to Lochranza route

Please keep dogs under control, and take extra care during the lambing and deer-calving season

Viewpoint in Brodick Country Park or Goatfell

Goatfell and neighbouring mountainous country gifted in 1958 by Lady Jean Fforde, daughter of Mary, Duchess of Montrose

Goatfell	All year		M T W T F S S

Bachelors' Club

Sandgate Street, Tarbolton, South Ayrshire KA5 5RB

tel 0844 493 2146
during opening times

A chance to find out more about Scotland's most famous poet, Robert Burns.

In this 17th-century thatched house, Burns attended dancing lessons in 1779. He formed a debating club here in 1780, and no doubt he and his friends would have heatedly discussed the topics of the day before drinking their fill at the inn next door. Burns was also initiated as a Freemason here in 1781.

£ E

OS Ref: NS431272
Road: In Tarbolton, off A77 10m S of Kilmarnock and off A76 at Mauchline, 7½m NE of Ayr **Bus:** ½-hourly from Ayr; (0871) 200 2233

Children's quizzes

Public parking outside house. Ground floor only

12 steps to upstairs room

On street outside property

Purchased in 1938

House	23 Mar to 30 Sep	1-5	M T . . F S S

Robert Burns Birthplace Museum

Murdoch's Lone, Alloway, Ayr KA7 4PQ

ROBERT
BURNS
BIRTHPLACE
MUSEUM

tel 0844 493 2601
fax 0844 493 2602
website www.burnsmuseum.org.uk

Robert Burns has become an international icon. His national pride, fierce egalitarianism and quick wit have become synonymous with the Scottish character itself. Set among 4 hectares of the poet's cherished Alloway countryside, Robert Burns Birthplace Museum offers you a truly unique encounter with Scotland's favourite son.

Main Exhibition
Not to be missed. A 21st-century monument to Burns and to the power of Scots language and song, this award-winning museum houses the world's best collection of Burns artefacts and original works, presented along with films and installations that bring Burns's legacy bursting to life.

Burns Cottage
The poet's birthplace has long been an international destination. Step under its thatched eaves or listen to the whispered tales and songs that ignited a remarkable childhood imagination.

Poet's Path
A connection between the poet's heritage and his power to inspire. See how contemporary artists and craftspeople have transformed the pathway into an open air gallery space.

Burns Monument
In sumptuous riverside gardens, heavy with the scent of roses and the music of birdsong, Burns Monument embodies the enduring love affair between the people of Alloway and their romantic hero.

Alloway Auld Kirk
Taste a little of the excitement and terror that Tam o' Shanter felt when you enter one of the most atmospheric and mysterious sites in Scotland.

Brig o' Doon
The River Doon and its medieval bridge form one of Scotland's most romantic beauty spots. Imagine the lovelorn young Burns composing *The Banks o' Doon* to the tune of its babbling waters.

Perfectly located within easy reach of Scotland's busiest cities and some beautiful coastal scenery, and less than 10 miles from an international airport, Robert Burns Birthplace Museum is an excellent destination for either a day out or as the ideal base for exploring Burns Country.

OS Ref: NS334185
Road: 2½m S of Ayr; signposted from A77 **Rail:** Ayr station, 2½m **Bus:** Stagecoach (X77); (01292) 61350

Hourly at weekends. Special tours available by advance request

Licensed self-service café at museum offering a wide range of freshly prepared home-cooked meals

Indoor and outdoor play areas, interactive displays, baby changing facilities at museum; children's holiday workshops and family activities

Accessible apart from Alloway Auld Kirk and exit from Burns Monument Gardens to Brig o' Doon

Induction loops

At museum and Burns Cottage

Adult £8, Family £20, 1 parent £16, Concession £6

Burns National Heritage Park gifted in 2008. Burns Cottage and Museum, Burns Monument and Gardens and partial ownership of the Brig o' Doon was transferred to the Trust from the Burns Monument Trust. Link walkway and land for site of new museum gifted by South Ayrshire Council

RBBM										
3 Jan to 31 Mar	10-5		M	T	W	T	F	S	S
1 Apr to 30 Sep	10-5.30		M	T	W	T	F	S	S
1 Oct to 31 Dec	10-5 (closed 25/26 Dec)		M	T	W	T	F	S	S

Culzean Castle & Country Park

Maybole, South Ayrshire KA19 8LE

tel 0844 493 2149
fax 0844 493 2150

group/school bookings, ranger service, country park information
tel 0844 493 2148
fax 0844 493 2151

Culzean is the perfect place for a day out for all the family – whether you're a keen walker, a gardener, interested in architecture or happy just to soak up some history. The castle was converted by the architect Robert Adam as a bachelor residence for the Earl of Cassillis between 1777 and 1792. Gazing across the Clyde from the Round Drawing Room, he must have been very pleased with the result. Our guides can tell you all about the best features of the house including Adam's masterpiece, the Oval Staircase, as well as the fine collection of paintings and furniture.

If you're hungry for military history, don't miss the Armoury with its impressive display of flintlock pistols and swords. There's also a strong link with President Eisenhower, as the top-floor apartment was presented to him for his lifetime in 1945 in recognition of his role during World War II. Nowadays, you can stay in the Eisenhower Apartment as a paying guest.

Out around the country park, miles of waymarked paths lead you on a voyage of discovery through majestic woodland and past secluded ponds.

Head for the Deer Park, the Cliff Top Walk or to the beaches. The more adventurous can seek out the landscape's hidden history through the ice houses, the Camellia House, the Pagoda or the caves. Gardeners can take inspiration from the magnificent and productive double Walled Garden, with its huge herbaceous borders and beautifully restored Victorian Vinery.

The perfect spot for a family picnic is the Swan Pond where children will also enjoy the adventure playground and a traditional dairy ice cream from the snack-bar. During your visit, don't miss the Visitor Centre where you can see our introductory film on Culzean, browse for gifts in the shop, revisit your childhood in the traditional toy shop or enjoy a tasty snack or meal in the Home Farm Restaurant.

Call for information about our programme of special events – everything from nature walks to Living History events, *al fresco* plays and magical Christmas events.

Culzean Country Park is managed in partnership with

£ A – Castle & Country Park

£ C – Country Park only

OS Ref: NS232103
Road: On A719, 12m S of Ayr, 4m W of Maybole **Cycle:** NCN 7
Bus: Stagecoach, Ayr to Girvan via Maidens (No 60). Bus stops at entrance. NB 1m walk downhill from bus stop to Castle/Visitor Centre
Rail: Maybole station, 4m

Guided tours of castle, 11am and 2.30pm daily. Family 11.30am on Sundays

Leaflet available

Old Smiddy Toy Shop, Visitor Centre Shop, Castle Shop, Traditional Sweetie Shop, Second-hand Bookshop

Licensed Visitor Centre restaurant, snack-bar at Swan Pond

Baby changing facilities, baby backpacks and pushchairs not allowed in castle, hip carrying system available; children's adventure playground, clubs for 6-12 year-olds and teenagers, children's activities

Please keep dogs away from deer park fence during calving in May/June. No dogs allowed in adventure playground

Civil wedding licence, exclusive dinners, private parties, receptions and marquee areas

Explanatory text: Dutch, French, German, Italian, Spanish
Multi-media guides: French, German, Spanish, Italian, Gaelic, BSL

Parking: at Visitor Centre, Deer Park and Walled Garden; in front of castle (for disabled drivers only, disabled passengers may be dropped off). Lifts in castle and Visitor Centre (limited access). Shop, restaurant, coffee shop, some parts of gardens and Country Park. Toilets. Manual wheelchairs and motorised scooters available (book in advance)

Large-print room guides. Tapping rails on some paths

Induction loop in auditorium

Visitor Centre: cars and buses; Deer Park: cars and buses; Walled Garden and Swan Pond: cars only – no bus access

Given by the 5th Marquess of Ailsa and the Kennedy family in 1945. The Country Park is managed by the Trust on behalf of a joint committee representing South Ayrshire Council and the National Trust for Scotland. Restored Dolphin House and new Bunkhouse leased to South Ayrshire Council as an Outdoor Education Centre

Country Park	All year	9.30-sunset		M T W T F S S
Walled Garden	All year	9.30-5 or sunset if earlier		M T W T F S S
Castle	28 Mar to 27 Oct	10.30-5 (last entry 4pm)		M T W T F S S
Visitor Centre	8 Jan to 24 Mar	11-4		. . . . . S S
	28 Mar to 31 Oct	10-5.30		M T W T F S S
	1 Nov to 31 Dec	11-4 (closed 28/29 Dec)		. . . . . S S

Souter Johnnie's Cottage

Main Road, Kirkoswald, South Ayrshire KA19 8HY

tel 0844 493 2147

A visit to Souter Johnnie's Cottage is like stepping into one of Burns's poems. This was the home of souter (shoemaker) John Davidson and his family. Souter Johnnie was immortalised by Burns in the poem *Tam o' Shanter* – 'and at his elbow, Souter Johnnie, his ancient, trusty, drouthy crony'.

The thatched cottage, built in 1785, is furnished in period style and contains Burns memorabilia. It also contains a workshop displaying the tools of a village souter.

In another cottage in the garden you'll find life-sized stone figures of the souter, Tam, the innkeeper and his wife sitting around the fire – much as Burns visualised them – 'fast by an ingle, bleezing finely'.

OS Ref: NS240075
Road: On A77, in Kirkoswald, 4m SW of Maybole **Cycle:** 4m from NCN 7 **Bus:** Frequent service from Ayr or Girvan

Family quiz book

Explanatory text: Dutch, French, German, Italian

Parking nearby on roadside. Easy access to cottage. Steep sloping garden

Free parking on main road or local authority car park at S end of village, c150 metres

Given in 1932 by the cottage's restoration trust

Cottage	23 Mar to 30 Sep	11.30-5	M T . . F S S

Greater Glasgow & Clyde Valley

web www.nts.org.uk

Weaver's Cottage

David Livingstone Centre

The Tenement House

National Museum of Rural Life

Glasgow

Pollok House

Holmwood

Greenbank Garden

Pollok House

Greenbank Garden

Flenders Road, Clarkston, Glasgow G76 8RB

tel 0844 493 2201
fax 0844 493 2200

If you're looking for ideas, inspiration and practical tips for your own garden, then a visit to Greenbank is a must. The 1ha (2.5a) walled garden in the grounds of Greenbank House has been designed to showcase new ideas and techniques for domestic gardens. There are 30 different areas to see, containing 3,600 named plants as well as important collections of *Narcissus* and *Bergenia*. Join us for a practical demonstration or a guided walk and you'll find your own gardening skills blossoming nicely.

2013 is Greenbank's 250th anniversary – check website for special events.

 D

OS Ref: NS561566
Road: Off A726 (signposted Greenbank Garden). Off M77 junction 4. Off A727 at Clarkston Toll (6m S of Glasgow city centre) **Cycle:** 4m from NCN 7, 75 **Bus:** No 44/44a, Glasgow to Newton Mearns; (0141) 333 3708 **Rail:** Clarkston station, 1¼m

Garden	All year	9.30-sunset	M T W T F S S
Shop and Tearoom	5 Jan to 22 Mar	1-4	. . . . . S S
	23 Mar to 23 Oct	11-5	M T W T F S S
	24 Oct to 19 Dec	1-4	. . . . . S S
House	23 Mar to 20 Oct	2-4	. . . . . . S

Guided tours available (also by arrangement for pre-booked groups)

Tearoom

Baby changing facilities, pushchairs in garden only, children's activities

Wedding ceremonies, private parties, receptions and marquee areas

Parking at reception. Shop, tearoom, walled garden. Toilets. Two wheelchairs available. Advice for disabled gardeners

Scented/textured plants in sections of garden

House and land gifted in 1976 by Mr & Mrs William Blyth

Holmwood

61-63 Netherlee Road, Cathcart, Glasgow G44 3YU

tel/fax 0844 493 2204

Discover this exquisite little gem – a classically inspired villa just a few miles from the centre of Glasgow. Completed in 1858, Holmwood is considered to be the finest domestic design by the architect Alexander 'Greek' Thomson. Inside this richly ornamented house there are exciting developments taking place. Come and watch the progress of our conservation experts as they reveal original stencilled wall decoration in the dining room, and discover more from the exhibition and audio tour. Appropriately, Holmwood is the base for the Alexander Thomson Society and there's an information and study centre dedicated to his work. There are 2 hectares (5a) of landscaped grounds to explore and a small kitchen garden, planted with a range of Victorian herbs, fruit and vegetables.

D ❄ Herbs

OS Ref: NS585597
Road: Netherlee Road, off Clarkston Road, B767 or Rhannan Road. 4m S of Glasgow city centre **Cycle:** 2m from NCN 7, 75 **Bus:** Frequent service from city centre along Clarkston Road **Rail:** Cathcart station, 1m

Max 15 people

'Greek' Thomson-related goods and books of architectural interest

Baby changing facilities, pushchairs in garden only, baby backpacks not allowed, children's quizzes

Audio tour: French, German

Parking at rear of property, wheelchair access at side. House fully accessible (lift). Toilet. Wheelchair available. Some of grounds accessible

Audio tour and room guides

Inductive ear hook for audio tour of house

Acquired from the Sisters of Our Lady of the Missions in 1994

House	23 Mar to 31 Oct	12-5		**M . . T F S S**

Morning visits for pre-booked groups.

National Museum of Rural Life

Wester Kittochside, Philipshill Road, East Kilbride, South Lanarkshire G76 9HR

National Museums Scotland

tel 0131 247 4377
email info@nms.ac.uk
website www.nms.ac.uk/rural

A day out at the National Museum of Rural Life gives you a unique opportunity to get back to the land and experience the traditional way of life on a Scottish farm. The farm itself is still worked using techniques and equipment from the 1950s. Whatever the season, there's always work to be done and you can see ploughing, sowing, haymaking and harvesting at different times of the year. Children will love the tractor trailer ride up to the Georgian farmhouse, where they'll get to meet the farm's dairy cows and sheep. In the exhibition centre, find out how people lived and worked the land in the past, and how they've shaped countryside as it is today.

OS Ref: NS608564
Road: From Glasgow take A727 to East Kilbride. From Edinburgh follow M8 to junction 6 on A725 to East Kilbride **Bus:** First Bus (No 31), Glasgow to East Kilbride, stops 200 metres from entrance **Rail:** Frequent service to East Kilbride station, 3m

By prior arrangement

Café

Baby changing facilities, children's activities, pushchairs allowed, baby backpacks allowed, play areas

Dogs allowed outside exhibition if on a lead

Parking at exhibition centre, drop-off point at farm. Farm and ground floor of farmhouse, exhibition centre, café, shop. Toilets. Wheelchairs available. Transport to farm

Large print leaflet and map of site

Induction loops in theatre and learning centre

Farm gifted by Mrs C S Reid in 1992. Additional land purchased in 1997

Museum	All year	10-5 (closed 25/26 Dec and 1 Jan)	**M T W T F S S**

Managed by NMS. Please note there may be a charge to Trust members for some events. Please telephone for details.

David Livingstone Centre

165 Station Road, Blantyre, South Lanarkshire G72 9BY

tel 0844 493 2207
fax 0844 493 2206

There can't be many people who have survived an attack by a lion. But Scotland's most famous explorer, Dr David Livingstone, is one of them. This incident, one of many remarkable events throughout his life, is dramatically re-created in a sculpture designed and gifted by the Oscar-winning animator Ray Harryhausen, and his wife Diana, Livingstone's great-granddaughter.

In 1813, Livingstone was born here in a single-roomed house in Shuttle Row, today a Grade A listed tenement. It is now part of a museum showing his extraordinary achievements. Find out how he grew from a lowly factory boy to become an African explorer and a hero of the Victorian age. The museum also gives a fascinating insight into the harsh conditions endured by industrial workers in the 19th century.

Many of Livingstone's personal belongings are on display including journals, and navigational and medical equipment – clearly he was not a man to travel light! His is an engaging story for all ages and for youngsters there's plenty to do – including quizzes, dressing up, and even a lion hunt.

Surrounded by ancient woodland, which has been designated a Site of Special Scientific Interest, the Centre is located in 8 hectares (20a) of wildlife-rich parkland, originally the Mill Manager's estate. The estate's garden has been regenerated and is now known as the Explorer's Garden, a peaceful, shady oasis bordered by the River Clyde. The more formal garden features the *World Fountain*, a recently refurbished water feature which was designed by renowned sculptor Pilkington Jackson in 1935. The Centre is also an ideal starting point for walks towards Bothwell Castle along the picturesque Clyde Walkway.

2013 is the bicentenary of David Livingstone's birth. See website for special events.

OS Ref: NS695584
Road: Just off M74, junction 5, via A725 and A724 **Cycle:** 1m from NCN 75 **Bus:** From Buchanan bus station, Glasgow, and East Kilbride **Rail:** Frequent service, Glasgow Central to Blantyre station, 5 mins' walk

By prior arrangement

Selection of gifts, including African crafts, books and toys

Tearoom

Baby changing facilities in Africa Pavilion, pushchair storage in Africa Pavilion (but they can be taken into museum), baby backpacks allowed, play area, family activities

Meeting facilities

Dogs are welcome in the park on a lead

Guidebook: French, German, Spanish. Explanatory text: Afrikaans, French, German, Italian, Spanish, Swahili

Car park c250 metres from Centre. Closer access by arrangement. Access to ground and upper floors (via lift). Toilet, shop, tearoom. Woodland garden accessible, although there are slopes

Transcripts of audio interpretation

Management of Centre transferred to the Trust in 1999 by the Governors of the Scottish National Memorial to David Livingstone Trust. Partnership formed between the Trust, the Governors, South Lanarkshire Council and Scottish Enterprise Lanarkshire to raise funds for operation and development of Centre

Centre	1 Mar* to 24 Dec	10-5 (Sun 12.30-5)	**M T W T F S S**

*The centre may open before this date, please check www.nts.org.uk or www.davidlivingstone200.org for more information

The Tenement House

145 Buccleuch Street, Garnethill, Glasgow G3 6QN

tel 0844 493 2197

'A real time capsule.' Just one of the comments from visitors who've been captivated by this unique property – an early 20th-century Glasgow tenement frozen in time. This first-floor apartment was the home of shorthand typist Miss Agnes Toward, who lived here for over 50 years. Little has changed since the turn of the 20th century, and you can see many of the original features such as the bed recesses, the kitchen range, coal bunker and bathroom. Listen to the hiss of the gas lights and the ticking of the grandfather clock and you'll be transported back in time. Our guides will be happy to tell you more about tenement life – many have lived in tenements themselves, and some still do.

E ⬜ £ D

OS Ref: NS581662
Road: From M8, junction 18 to Sauchiehall Street. First left into Garnet Street, then 3rd left into Buccleuch Street **Cycle:** 1m from NCN 7, 75
Bus: First Bus; (0141) 423 6600
Underground: Cowcaddens station
Rail: Charing Cross station, Elmbank Street to Sauchiehall Street; then see road directions (above)

➡ For groups, by prior arrangement

Baby changing facilities, pushchairs must be left at reception, object handling collection, children's quiz

Guidebook: French, Italian. Explanatory text: Dutch, French, German, Italian, Japanese, Spanish

Many steps in house

Braille guidebook. Object handling collection. Large-print information sheet

Induction loop

P Limited parking outside house using vouchers (available to buy at reception)

A Purchased in 1982

House | 1 Mar to 31 Oct | 1-5 | **M T W T F S S**

Weaver's Cottage

The Cross, Kilbarchan, Renfrewshire PA10 2JG

tel 0844 493 2205

With original working looms and spinning wheels, the traditional weaver's craft comes vividly to life. Built in 1723, the weaver's cottage houses the last of 800 handlooms once working in the village of Kilbarchan. The weavers today use the 200-year-old loom, specialising in the making of tartan. They can explain how wool and flax were coloured using natural dyes, many of which are obtained from plants and herbs in the pretty cottage garden. You too can try your hand at weaving, pirn winding and spinning – guides are always on hand to help. Stories about archaeological digs in the garden, local history research documents and a DVD presentation on the village's involvement in the making of Paisley shawls are also available.

E ⬜ ⛩ £ D

OS Ref: NS401634
Road: M8, junction 28A, A737, follow signs for Kilbarchan. 12m SW of Glasgow **Cycle:** 1m from NCN 7, 75
Bus: Frequent service from Paisley, Glasgow and from Johnstone rail station (2m) passes door

Children's activities, baby backpacks allowed, storage for pushchairs

Objects to handle. Scented plants in garden

Subtitled audio-visual programme

P Free public car park, 100 metres

A Given in 1954 by the family of Miss Christie, the last handloom weaver in the house

Cottage | 23 Mar to 30 Sep | 1-5 | **M T . . F S S**

A bonus for art lovers is the superb collection of paintings. Here you can see works by El Greco, Blake and Murillo.

Pollok House

Pollok Country Park, 2060 Pollokshaws Road, Glasgow G43 1AT

tel 0844 493 2202
fax 0844 493 2203

Step into the magnificent mahogany and marble hallway at Pollok House and it's hard to believe you're only a few miles from Glasgow's vibrant city centre. The ancestral home of the Maxwell family who lived on the site for over six centuries, the present house was begun in the mid-18th century and extended in the Victorian period. The interiors at Pollok House are fabulous and visitors will be delighted by the period furnishings, silverware and ceramics on display. A bonus for art lovers is the superb collection of Spanish paintings. Here you can see works by El Greco, Goya and Murillo. Also on view are works by the English artist and poet William Blake.

Carry on to the servants' quarters and you'll get a clear picture of the scale of operations needed to keep the house running. Look out for the Victorian photograph of the household staff and count up the number of servants! At certain times of the year the house is miraculously brought back to life as 'staff' and 'family members' in period costume go about their business. A vivid and entertaining glimpse into the past.

After all that, perhaps you're ready for a bite to eat. Head for our award-winning Edwardian Kitchen Restaurant for a spot of lunch or a taste of home baking. You can also experience a unique shopping adventure. So come and step back in time and discover a wide range of specialist fine foods and exclusive gifts in our food and gift shops, especially at Christmas time.

There's always something going on at Pollok House. Christmas celebrations are magical when the house is beautifully decorated and Mrs Claus is in residence! At Easter we welcome Mrs Cotton Tail. And there's a murder mystery every day in July and August for you to solve. There are educational events and school programmes for children too. Don't forget there are a number of rooms available to hire for weddings, conferences and other functions.

Road: Off M77, junctions 1 or 2, follow signs for Burrell Collection, 3m S of Glasgow city centre
Cycle: NCN 7, 75 **Bus/Rail:** Frequent bus and rail (Pollokshaws West station 200 metres from Country Park entrance) from Glasgow city centre.

Max 15 people. Please book in advance (£2 per person)

In country park

Gift shop, bookshop, food shop

Licensed restaurant and tea garden (staff permitting)

Baby changing facilities, buggy park for prams and junior bikes, baby backpacks not allowed, children's quizzes, events

Parts or all of the property may be closed during normal opening hours due to functions. Certain special event charges apply to Trust members too. Please contact the property before you visit

Civil wedding licence, exclusive dinners, private parties, receptions and marquee areas

Explanatory text: French, German, Italian, Spanish, Dutch, Japanese, Polish, Urdu

Parking outside house. Accessible entrance via road to right of building. Stairlift and lift to main floor rooms. Restaurant, tearoom, shops. Toilet. Wheelchair available

Two steps to front hall, steps to main rooms upstairs

Large-print room guides available from reception

D. But free entry from 1 Nov to 31 Mar, although there may be a charge for certain events

House managed in partnership with Glasgow City Council since 1998

			M	T	W	T	F	S	S
Garden and Country Park All year			M	T	W	T	F	S	S
House, Shops and Restaurant	All year	10-5 (closed 25/26 Dec and 1/2 Jan)	M	T	W	T	F	S	S

Entry to the Servants' corridor, all shops and the Edwardian Kitchen Restaurant is free throughout the year.

Adam Naming the Beasts by William Blake, at Pollok House

Craignure

Oban

Crianlarich

A85

A85

A82

A827

Arduaine Garden

Ben Lomond

Crarae Garden

Stirling

The Hill House

Helensburgh

Geilston Garden

Glasgow

A811

M80

A8

Arduaine Garden

Arduaine, Oban, Argyll PA34 4XQ

tel/fax 0844 493 2216

Any time is a good time to visit Arduaine Garden, a tranquil green oasis nestling at the foot of the Arduaine peninsula on the west coast south of Oban, and to enjoy the delights of the neighbouring Loch Melfort Hotel, originally Arduaine House.

The garden will surprise and delight visitors all year round. This south-facing garden on the Sound of Jura benefits from the warming effect of the North Atlantic Drift, and can be spectacular in springtime. Proximity to the sea allows the cultivation of many rare and tender plants from around the globe, with the emphasis on South America and East Asia. The renowned rhododendron collection attracts enthusiasts from far and wide, and azaleas, magnolias and many other shrubs and trees fill the garden with scent and colour. Blue Tibetan poppies, Chatham Island forget-me-nots and giant Himalayan lilies are just part of the perennial collection, flowering well into autumn; carniverous plants, palms and ferns, including tree ferns, add to a sense of the exotic.

While at Arduaine, take time to explore the adjacent Loch Melfort Hotel, now working in close partnership with the Trust. This very comfortable Scottish country house hotel dates back to 1896 and retains many original features, so is full of character and warmth. It's a perfect base to discover the delights of the west coast around Oban, or if you are just visiting for the day, the hotel offers a wide range of meals and snacks. Choose from either the Chartroom II Bistro, with its locally sourced food and spectacular sea views, or the more formal Asknish Bay Restaurant (AA 2 rosettes). Arduaine is a haven for wildlife, so look out for kestrels, seals, otters and porpoises. For younger visitors, don't miss the Highland cattle, sheep, hens and ducks in the hotel grounds, as well as enjoying the play park and a walk to the sandy beach. Further details from Calum and Rachel Ross, tel 01852 200233 or visit www.lochmelfort.co.uk.

OS Ref: NM794103
Road: A816, 20m S of Oban and 19m N of Lochgilphead **Bus:** Infrequent service passes entrance; West Coast Motors (015850) 552319

Charge made

Seeds from garden for sale

At Loch Melfort Hotel bistro

Children's guide, play area (Loch Melfort Hotel)

Well behaved dogs on a short lead allowed in garden

Civil wedding licence, exclusive dinners, private parties, receptions

Loch Melfort Hotel

Brief information sheet: French, German, Spanish, Italian, Dutch

Accessible path from car park. Some of garden accessible with assistance. Wheelchair available. Toilet

Scented flowers

£ Adult £6, Family £16, 1 parent £11, Concession £5. Tickets are available from Garden Reception between 9.30-4.30 every day from Apr to Sep. **Outwith these times**, please purchase your tickets from the Chartroom II Bistro at the adjacent Loch Melfort Hotel

A Garden gifted to the Trust in 1992 by Edmund and Harry Wright

Garden	All year	9.30-sunset	M T W T F S S
Reception Centre	23 Mar to 30 Sep	9.30-4.30	M T W T F S S

< Arduaine Garden

Ben Lomond

Ardess Lodge, Rowardennan, by Drymen G63 0AR

tel 0844 493 2217

Rising from the east shore of Loch Lomond to a height of 974m (3193ft), Ben Lomond offers exhilarating walking and spectacular views across Loch Lomond & the Trossachs National Park. Walks range in difficulty from an arduous but rewarding ascent to the summit of Ben Lomond, to the leisurely Ardess Hidden History Trail – a low-level walk the whole family can enjoy. Details on walks and other information are available from the display trailer, located either at Rowardennan car park or at the Ben Lomond ranger centre at Ardess Lodge. Why not enhance your group visit by pre-booking a ranger as a guide? They'll be able to tell you all about this magnificent terrain and the vital conservation work that's going on, and help keep you on the right path!

OS Ref: NS367029
Road: B837 at Rowardennan, 11m beyond Drymen, off A811 **Cycle:** Near NCN 7 **Rail:** Glasgow to Balloch then **Bus:** Glasgow-Drymen-Balmaha, then 7m walk/cycle to Rowardennan **Ferry:** Luss or Tarbet to Rowardennan, details from www.cruiselochlomond.co.uk or 01301 702356

Ardess Lodge bunkhouse, contact property or holidays department for details

Sheep farming area, please keep dogs under control at all times

Parking at Rowardennan car park. Car access to Ranger Centre by arrangement. Small ramp into lobby of Centre. Toilets

Pay & Display at Rowardennan car park (Forestry Commission)

Purchased in 1984. Forms part of the Ben Lomond National Memorial Park and the Loch Lomond & the Trossachs National Park

Ben Lomond	All year		M T W T F S S

Crarae Garden

Crarae, Inveraray, Argyll PA32 8YA

tel/fax 0844 493 2210 (Visitor Centre)

Standing among the exotic trees and shrubs on the hillside at Crarae, listening to the tumbling waterfalls of the burn, you could almost imagine you're in the Himalayas, rather than Argyll. The glen-side layout of mature woody plants and informal paths radiates from the burn and creates a wonderfully natural effect. The garden was first started by Grace, Lady Campbell in 1912 and includes a National Collection of *Nothofagus*, or southern beech, as well as superb examples of *Acer*, *Sorbus*, *Eucryphia* and *Eucalyptus*. From the early flowers of countless rhododendrons, azaleas, camellias and magnolias to the rich autumn tints of foliage and fruit, it's a magical spot at any time of year.

OS Ref: NR986973
Road: A83, 10m S of Inveraray **Bus:** Infrequent services from Inveraray and Lochgilphead; West Coast Motors (01586) 552319

By prior arrangement, £25 for max group of 12

Hot and cold drinks, and prepacked snacks

Baby changing facilities, baby backpacks allowed, storage for pushchairs

Dogs on a short lead allowed

Parking at entrance. Visitor Centre, refreshment area, shop. Lower garden and viewing platform in glen accessible with assistance. Steps and steep slopes elsewhere. Toilet. Wheelchair available

Induction loop

Gifted in 2002 by the Crarae Garden Charitable Trust, following a successful £1.5 million appeal

Garden	All year	9.30-sunset	M T W T F S S
Visitor Centre	23 Mar to 31 Jul	10-5	M T W T F S S
	1 Aug to 31 Oct	10-5	M . . T F S S

Geilston Garden

Main Road, Cardross, Dumbarton G82 5HD

tel 0844 493 2219
fax 0844 493 2220

Geilston is an intimate and tranquil garden best enjoyed at an unhurried pace. On entering the walled garden, the giant Wellingtonia tree will instantly impress, as will the spring displays of azaleas, followed in summer by colour on a grand scale in the herbaceous border. From here, wander into the woodland garden complete with waterfall, bridges over the Geilston Burn and mossy paths. Beneath the tree canopy, the pathways are carpeted in spring with wood anemones and bluebells. Make your way to the kitchen garden and feast your eyes on the wide range of fresh produce grown, some of which you can buy in season – so you can eat and conserve!

🖊 🌳 **P** **£** D

✕ **OS Ref:** NS340783
Road: On A814 at W end of Cardross, 18m NW of Glasgow **Cycle:** 3m from NCN 7 **Bus:** ½-hourly service from Helensburgh to Dumbarton passes entrance to drive **Rail:** Glasgow to Helensburgh, ½-hourly service, to Cardross station, 1m

➡ By prior arrangement, £1 per person (min £20)

🍴 Hot drinks

❗ Only assistance dogs allowed in garden

♿ Garden accessible with assistance. Toilet

A Bequeathed in 1989 by Miss E C Hendry

Garden	23 Mar to 31 Oct	9.30-5	M T W T F S S

The Hill House

Upper Colquhoun Street, Helensburgh G84 9AJ

tel 0844 493 2208
fax 0844 493 2209

A masterpiece of domestic architecture designed by Charles Rennie Mackintosh, The Hill House was built for the Glasgow publisher Walter Blackie and his family between 1902 and 1904. With beautiful views over the Clyde Estuary, the house blends tradition with a uniquely modern twist and is as visually striking today as it was a hundred years ago. The stunning interior is a result of collaborations between Mackintosh and his wife, Margaret Macdonald, who contributed fabric designs and the beautiful 'Sleeping Princess' gesso panel in the drawing room.

The gardens have also been restored and round off any visit to the house. Mackintosh laid out the broad lines of the garden and suggested details such as the lilac circle to the east, although it was the Blackies who shaped the garden you see today.

E **£** C

✕ **OS Ref:** NS300838
Road: On eastern edge of Helensburgh. Off A818, between A82 and A814, 23m NW of Glasgow **Rail:** ½-hourly service, Glasgow to Helensburgh, then 1½m walk or taxi

🛍 Vibrant design shop selling unique items by contemporary designers. Second shop specialises in Mackintosh-inspired goods, and books of architectural and historical interest

🍴 Tearoom

👶 Baby backpacks allowed, pushchairs ground floor and garden only, storage for pushchairs, children's quiz

🔲 Explanatory text: French, German, Italian, Japanese, Spanish, Russian

♿ Parking next to house. Limited access at house. Garden partially accessible. Toilet

↕ Steps to entrance and internal stairs

👁 Braille guidebook and information sheets

P Car park to rear of the house; please do not park on the street

A Donated in 1982 by the Hill House Trustees with the approval of the Royal Incorporation of Architects in Scotland

House	23 Mar to 31 Oct	1.30-5.30	M T W T F S S

Morning visits for pre-booked groups.

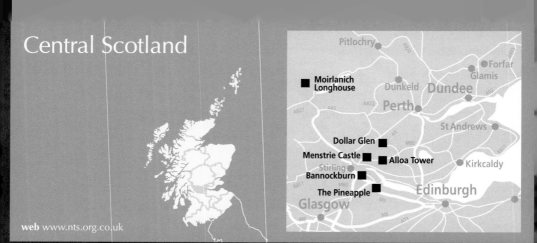

Central Scotland

Moirlanich
Longhouse

Pitlochry

Forfar
Glamis

Dunkeld
Dundee

Perth

St Andrews

Dollar Glen

Menstrie Castle
Alloa Tower

Stirling
Bannockburn
Kirkcaldy

The Pineapple

Edinburgh

Glasgow

web www.nts.org.co.uk

Alloa Tower

Alloa Park, Alloa, Clackmannanshire FK10 1PP

tel 0844 493 2129
fax 0844 493 2131

Dating from the 14th century, Alloa Tower is the largest, oldest keep in Scotland. The Tower was the ancestral home of the Erskine family, the Earls of Mar and Kellie. The Erskines were loyal supporters of several Stuart monarchs who spent part of their early lives in Alloa Tower, including Mary, Queen of Scots and James VI and I. As the family rose to prominence they played a little known but important part in many episodes of Scottish history. The Tower has been altered over the centuries and is now an 18th-century mansion contained within a medieval shell. Unusual features include a sweeping Italianate staircase, a rare double groin-vaulted ceiling, a magnificent medieval oak-beamed roof, and a medieval dungeon and 1st floor well. There is a collection of paintings and silver loaned by the Earl of Mar and Kellie.

E **P** **£** D

OS Ref: NS888924
Road: Off A907, in Alloa, close to town centre **Cycle:** 1m from NCN 76
Bus: Mackie's Coaches stop in town centre, then short walk;
(01259) 216180

By prior arrangement. Max 50 people

Baby changing facilities, not suitable for pushchairs/prams, quizzes, costumes, games, toys

Civil wedding licence

Parking at door by arrangement. Ground floor accessible. Slides of portraits. Toilet

Stairs to Great Hall on 1st floor. Narrow steep spiral staircase with handrail to remaining floors and roof-walk

Large-print interpretation

Audio-visual presentation with induction loop and subtitles

A Managed by the Trust since 1996 in partnership with Clackmannanshire Heritage Trust

Tower										
	23 Mar to 29 Apr	1-5		**M**	.	.	.	**F**	**S**	**S**
	3 May to 31 Aug	1-5		**M**	.	.	**T**	**F**	**S**	**S**
	1 Sep to 28 Oct	1-5		**M**	.	.	.	**F**	**S**	**S**

Last admission 45 mins before closing.
Visits outside these dates/times for pre-booked groups by arrangement with property.

< John Erskine, 6th Earl of Mar

Bannockburn

As you gaze across the field at
Bannockburn, listen carefully and
you might hear the cries of battle
echoing down the centuries…

Bannockburn

Glasgow Road, Stirling FK7 0LJ

tel 0844 493 2139
fax 0844 493 2138

This atmospheric spot is the site of Robert the Bruce's famous victory over the English. Here, in 1314, Bruce gathered his men to take on the army of King Edward II. Despite facing a greater number of professional troops, Bruce's men routed the English forces – a victory that meant freedom for Scotland from oppressive English rule. The sense of history here is tangible and Bannockburn is still a focus for Scottish pride today.

Walk the battlefield under the gaze of Robert the Bruce himself, immortalised in a statue by Pilkington Jackson.

In 2004, archaeologists found an iron arrowhead on Trust land that could well have been fired at the Battle of Bannockburn. This has caused great excitement as it's the only weapon to be recovered from the battlefield.

The Bannockburn Heritage Centre has closed to make way for a state-of-the-art visitor experience opening in 2014. A temporary information unit is on site. **Access to the site may be restricted at times, please check the website or telephone before visiting.**

The National Trust for Scotland and Historic Scotland are leading a unique project to revitalise the visitor experience at Bannockburn and mark the 700th anniversary of the Battle of Bannockburn.

The team will work with Historic Scotland's partners at Glasgow School of Art's Digital Design Studio to build an innovative digital exhibition that will give visitors a unique understanding of what it would have been like to be at Bannockburn 700 years ago.

Plans for activities and events are underway. The official opening of the new centre will be on 24 June 2014.

FREE

OS Ref: NS797905
Road: Off M80/M9 at junction 9, on A872, 2m S of Stirling **Bus:** Stirling bus station, First buses (Nos 24, 54, X39) or City Sightseeing Stirling open-top bus from Jun-Sep **Rail:** Stirling station, 2m

Dogs welcome in park

Guidebook: French, German, Polish

Parking.

Large print interpretation

Car park is closed in December and January

Presented to the Trust in 1932 by the Bannockburn Preservation Committee under the 10th Earl of Elgin and Kincardine, head of the Bruce family. Further land purchased in 1960 and 1965 to facilitate access

Site	All year	Until dusk (car park closed Dec & Jan)	M	T	W	T	F	S	S
Temporary Exhibition	1 Mar to 31 Mar	10-5	M	T	W	T	F	S	S
	1 Apr to 30 Sep	10-5.30	M	T	W	T	F	S	S

Dollar Glen

Dollar, Clackmannanshire

tel 0844 493 2133
(Greenbank House)

This wooded glen provides spectacular walks to Castle Campbell (see page 124). Dollar Glen has been designated a Site of Special Scientific Interest because of its range of wildlife habitats and important geological features.

Take care during or after rain as the paths can be dangerous.

OS Ref: NS961993
Road: Off A91, in Dollar **Bus:** Regular service from Stirling; (01324) 613777

Dogs must be kept under control during lambing season in spring and summer

(not National Trust for Scotland)

Glen and castle given in 1950 by Mr J E Kerr, CBE, of Harviestoun

Glen	All year	M T W T F S S

Menstrie Castle

Castle Street, Menstrie, Clackmannanshire

tel 0844 493 2129
(Alloa Tower)

Menstrie Castle was originally home to a branch of the Clan MacAlister, who later anglicised their name to Alexander. The castle was the birthplace of Sir William Alexander, who became 1st Earl of Stirling and later was James VI's Lieutenant for the Plantation of Nova Scotia. An exhibition in the Nova Scotia Commemoration Room tells the story

of this ill-fated scheme. The castle was also the birthplace of Sir Ralph Abercromby (1734-1801).

Although it's not a Trust property, the Trust worked closely with the then Clackmannanshire County Council to save the castle from demolition.

£ FREE

OS Ref: NS850967
Road: Off A91, in Menstrie, 5m NE of Stirling

Children's quizzes

Two steps into castle, remaining two rooms on level

Castle	Easter Sunday and 3 May to 30 Sep	2-5	. . W . . . S

Visits outside these dates/times for pre-booked groups by arrangement with Alloa Tower.

Moirlanich Longhouse

Near Killin, Stirling FK21 8UA

tel 0844 493 2136
(NTS office)

Visit this perfectly preserved cruck frame cottage and get a glimpse of rural life in the 20th century. Moirlanich was home to at least three generations of the Robertson family, with the last member leaving in 1968. The building has hardly been changed and retains many of its original features, such as the 'hingin' lum' and box beds. Next door there's an unusual collection of working clothes and 'Sunday best' which were discovered in the longhouse, and an exhibition on the history and restoration of the building.

E £ ᴱ

OS Ref: NN562342
Road: On Glen Lochay Road, off A827, 1m NW of Killin **Cycle:** 1m from NCN 7

Reception building but not longhouse. Toilet

P Limited, unsuitable for coaches

A Purchased in 1992 following a generous donation in memory of Sheriff Prain, from his family

Longhouse	Easter Sunday and 1 May to 30 Sep	2-5	. . W . . . S

Last entry 30 mins before closing. (Staffed by volunteers from Killin Heritage Society)

The Pineapple

N of Airth, Falkirk

tel 0844 493 2132

This bizarre structure, in the shape of a pineapple, was built around 1761 as a folly to enjoy the fantastic views.

Extensive glasshouses and pineapple pits once grew a variety of exotic fruits and vegetables within these walls. Ongoing research, survey and repair work continues on the walls and is revealing a great deal of information for future consideration.

The policies are now an oasis for wildlife. Enjoy a peaceful walk around the former curling and dipping pool and surrounding woodland. There is an all-ability path which leads from the car park to a pond viewing platform, where, if you are lucky, you may catch a glimpse of the rare great crested newt.

The Trust maintains the grounds and structures, and the building is leased to the Landmark Trust.

⛩ P

OS Ref: NS889884
Road: 7m E of Stirling, off A905, then off B9124. 1m W of Airth

Landmark Trust, Shottesbrooke, Maidenhead, Berks; (01628) 825925

Good views of the structure from a car. Picnic area in grounds

A Given with 6.5ha of gardens and policies in 1974 by the Countess of Perth. Acceptance was made possible by the co-operation of the Landmark Trust, which has leased and restored the building for short-term lets

Site	All year	9.30-sunset	M T W T F S S

Perthshire

Killiecrankie
Craigower
Pitlochry
Linn of Tummel
The Hermitage
Ben Lawers
Dunkeld
Dunkeld
Glamis
Forfar
Dundee
Perth
A9
A93
A90
A924
A827
A85
A822
A92
Branklyn Garden
A9
St Andrews
M90
Stirling
Kirkcaldy

Ben Lawers National Nature Reserve

NTS Office, Lynedoch, Main Street, Killin FK21 8UW

tel/fax 0844 493 2136

At 1,214m (3,984ft) Ben Lawers, the highest mountain in the central Highlands, gives its name to this internationally important reserve. Renowned for its rich arctic-alpine flora, it includes the southern slopes and summits of seven mountains in the Ben Lawers and Tarmachan ranges. From the summit of Ben Lawers itself you can get fantastic views over to Ben Lomond and Glencoe in the west and the high Cairngorms to the north, and there are a variety of scenic walking routes. Most of these are suitable for experienced walkers with the right equipment, but there are gentler routes too. The Edramucky Trail, which is ideal for families, provides the opportunity to experience a wealth of plants and wildlife in an area where pioneering conservation work has restored natural plant communities to the mountain. Insects such as moths and other invertebrates quickly colonised these recovering habitats, providing food for birds such as whinchat, stonechat and willow warblers. Higher up the mountain you may see red deer, ravens, ring ouzels and ptarmigan. During the summer, the ranger staff offer a programme of guided walks for visitors of all ages.

Site All year **M T W T F S S**

E ♦ ♦ £ F

⊠ **OS Ref:** NN608377
Road: Car park, 2m up hill road off A827, 6m NE of Killin, N of Loch Tay **Cycle:** Near NCN 7 **Bus:** Services to Killin (infrequent) and summer services along A827 with stops by request **Train:** Nearest stations at Crianlarich (20 miles), Pitlochry (35 miles), Stirling (45 miles) **Foot:** Access from A827 at NN614361

❗ Please keep dogs under control at all times

♿ Parking. Interpretation and some paths accessible with assistance (stone cobbles)

P Access unsuitable for coaches

A Bought in 1950 by the Trust's Mountainous Country Fund, formed by Percy Unna. Tarmachan range bought in 1996. Management of the National Nature Reserve is financially supported by Scottish Natural Heritage

Scotland's National Nature Reserves

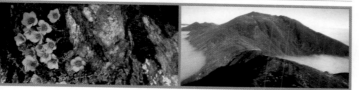

Branklyn Garden

116 Dundee Road, Perth PH2 7BB

tel 0844 493 2193

This attractive garden, a haven of peace within walking distance of Perth, was developed by John and Dorothy Renton with the help of seed collections from plant hunters such as Forrest, Ludlow and Sherriff. Gardeners and botanists from all over the world come to Branklyn to see the outstanding collection of plants, particularly rhododendrons, alpines, herbaceous and peat-garden plants. One of the most striking and unusual plants here is the vivid blue Himalayan poppy, *Meconopsis*. Branklyn also holds National Collections of *Cassiope* and *Lilium* (Mylnefield lilies), and is developing a collection of *Rhododendron taliense*.

Garden	23 Mar to 31 Oct	10-5	M T W T F S S
Shop	23 Mar to 30 Apr	10-5	M T . . F S S
	1 May to 30 Jun	10-5	M T W T F S S
	1 Jul to 30 Sep	10-5	M T . . F S S

🎁 ❄ → £ D

⊠ **OS Ref:** NO125225
Road: A85, Dundee Road, N of Perth, over Queen's Bridge, turn right and look for sign to car park on the left. From the N, via A90, follow signs to car park **Cycle:** close to NCN 77 **Bus:** Stagecoach (No 16) stops 200 metres from garden **Rail:** Perth station, 25 mins' walk

🚼 Baby changing facilities

❗ No dogs allowed in garden, but they can be left at gate

♿ Parking at entrance by arrangement with shop staff. Half of garden, shop. Toilet. Wheelchair available. Gravel paths

P 400 metres from entrance

A Bequeathed in 1967 by John T Renton, CBE, who, with his wife, began the garden planting in 1922

< Branklyn Garden

Craigower

Near Pitlochry, Perthshire

tel 0844 493 2192
(Perthshire Area Office) or
tel 0844 493 2194
(Killiecrankie Visitor Centre)

The climb to the top of Craigower (the Goat's Crag), at 407m (1,335ft), is certainly worth the stretch for the outstanding views of the surrounding National Scenic Area. On a clear day you can take in the views along Lochs Tummel and Rannoch to the distant hills of Glencoe.

The 4.5ha property consists of open heathland with scattered Scots pines and is locally important for butterflies, with fourteen species recorded, including the Green Hairstreak in spring and the Scotch Argus in late summer.

OS Ref: NN925604
Road: Off A924 at Moulin, 1½m N of Pitlochry **Cycle:** 1m from NCN 7
Rail: Pitlochry station, c2m

On Pitlochry footpath network, Craigower walk 6m from Pitlochry car parks, 3m from Craigower car park

c1.5m

Given in 1947 by Mrs M D Fergusson of Baledmund in memory of her father, Capt G A K Wisely

Site	All year	**M T W T F S S**

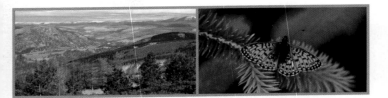

Dunkeld

Perthshire Area Office, 11 The Cross, Dunkeld, Perthshire PH8 0AN

tel 0844 493 2192
Ell Shop
tel 0844 493 2191

Nestling beneath thickly wooded hills alongside the River Tay, Dunkeld has an air of timeless tranquillity. In Cathedral Street and The Cross, the Trust has restored 20 houses, some dating from the rebuilding of the town after the Battle of Dunkeld in 1689. Although these private homes aren't open to the public, you're welcome at the Ell Shop, named after the weaver's measure on the wall outside.

Stanley Hill. An important remnant of the landscape around the original Dunkeld House, this early 18th-century terraced viewpoint is still easily accessible today.
Banks of Tay and Braan. The mile-long section along the south banks of the Rivers Tay and Braan provides a backdrop to Dunkeld Cathedral and the town. Part of the Birnam Circular Walk.

OS Ref: NO025427
Road: Off A9, 12m N of Perth
Cycle: NCN 77 **Bus:** Stagecoach; (01738) 629339 **Rail:** Dunkeld & Birnam station, 1m

On Dunkeld footpath network, covering c30m of waymarked paths

Small step into Ell Shop

Subtitled video in Tourist Information Centre

Pay & Display

Houses presented in 1954 by Atholl Estates; Stanley Hill in 1958 by Messrs J Jones (Larbert) Ltd; riverbanks in 1985 by the 10th Duke of Atholl; Atholl Memorial Fountain in 1989 by Dunkeld community

Shop	23 Mar to 31 Oct	10-5.30 (Sun 12.30-5.30)	**M T W T F S S**
	1 Nov to 23 Dec	10-4.30 (Sun 12.30-4.30)	**M T W T F S S**

Closed for 30 mins at lunchtime.

The Hermitage >>

The Hermitage
Near Dunkeld, Perthshire

tel 0844 493 2192
(Perthshire Area Office)

An attractive woodland walk leads along the banks of the River Braan, through mixed woodland and past a handsome single-arched bridge to the picturesque folly of Ossian's Hall. Overlooking the Black Linn Falls and beyond to Ossian's Cave, the mid-18th-century Hall was a focal point in an extensive designed landscape. Don't miss the exciting installation of contemporary art re-interpreting Ossian's Hall by artist Calum Colvin.

Today, it competes with the tumbling River Braan and some spectacularly tall Douglas fir trees, including one of Britain's tallest at over 64m (210ft). Each season offers something special – the striking contrast between the coniferous and deciduous trees in spring and autumn, the salmon attempting to jump the Falls in late summer, and, in winter, the temperature can turn the river into a glistening ice floe.

E 🚶 ⛵ P £ F

✕ **OS Ref:** NO008417
Road: Off A9, 2m W of Dunkeld
Cycle: 1m from NCN 77
Bus: Stagecoach, request stop at Inver; (01738) 629339 **Foot:** On Dunkeld footpath network, Inver walk (5m) and Braan walk (3¾m)

🚶 1½m circular walk

🍴 Apr-Oct only

💍 Wedding ceremonies

❗ Keep dogs under control at all times, and pick up and remove your dog's waste

♿ Parking at Ossian's Hall for disabled badge holders. Accessible path from car park to Hall, with one steeper gradient section

Ⓐ By the wish of the 8th Duke of Atholl, first president of the Trust, presented by his widow, Katharine, Duchess of Atholl, in 1944

Site	All year	M T W T F S S

Killiecrankie

Pitlochry, Perthshire PH16 5LG

tel 0844 493 2194
(Visitor Centre) or

tel 0844 493 2192
(Perthshire Area Office)

'The Pass is extremely narrow between high mountains, with the Garry running beneath in a deep, dark fome, and a rocky channel overhung with trees, forming a scene of horrible grandeur' wrote Thomas Pennant in 1769. This magnificent wooded gorge is a Site of Special Scientific Interest and lies within the Tummel National Scenic Area. Although tranquil now, on 27 July 1689 Killiecrankie echoed with the sound of gunfire when a Jacobite army led by 'Bonnie Dundee' defeated government forces. One soldier escaped by making a spectacular jump across the River Garry at the spot now known as Soldier's Leap. The Visitor Centre exhibition features seasonally changing interactive wildlife displays and children's activities, and tells the story of the battle, showing examples of the weapons used.

Visit www.bungeejumpscotland.co.uk to find out about bungee jumping at Killiecrankie.

OS Ref: NN917627
Road: B8079, 3m N of Pitlochry
Cycle: On NCN 7 **Bus:** Elizabeth Yule local service from Pitlochry; (01796) 472290 **Foot:** On Pitlochry footpath network, Killiecrankie walk (1¾m), Bealach walk (10¾m) **Rail:** Pitlochry station 3m, Blair Atholl station 4m

Footpath through Pass (1¼m). Uneven, steep and rough steps

Café, mainly take-away

Baby changing facilities

Keep dogs under control at all times in Pass and on leads around Centre

Explanatory text: Danish, French, Gaelic, German, Italian, Japanese, Swedish, Spanish, Polish, Russian

Visitor Centre, exhibition, shop, viewing balcony. Toilet

Objects to touch in exhibition. Large-print exhibition text

16ha of the Pass gifted in 1947 by Edith Foster. A further 1.2ha gifted in 1965 by Mr J Fergusson

Site	All year		M T W T F S S
Visitor Centre	23 Mar to 31 Oct	10-5.30	M T W T F S S

Linn of Tummel

Near Pitlochry, Perthshire

tel 0844 493 2192
(Perthshire Area Office) or
tel 0844 493 2195

Enjoy a peaceful wooded walk to the place where the Rivers Garry and Tummel meet. The Linn of Tummel – from the Gaelic *linne*, meaning pool – is a picturesque combination of water and woodland, and is home to a rich variety of wildlife. The area was favoured by Queen Victoria and an obelisk commemorates her visit here in 1844. Look out for the early example of a fish-pass (1910) beside the Linn which allowed salmon to bypass the Falls of Tummel on their way upstream.

OS Ref: NN910600
Road: B8019, 2½m NW of Pitlochry
Cycle: Just off NCN 7 **Bus:** Elizabeth Yule local service, Pitlochry to Garry Bridge; (01796) 472290 **Foot:** On Pitlochry footpath network, Killiecrankie walk (1½m), starting at Pitlochry

Circular walk from Garry Bridge car park

Keep dogs under control at all times

Garry Bridge car park. Free

Given in 1944 by Dr G F Barbour of Bonskeid

Site	All year		M T W T F S S

House of Dun ≫

Angus

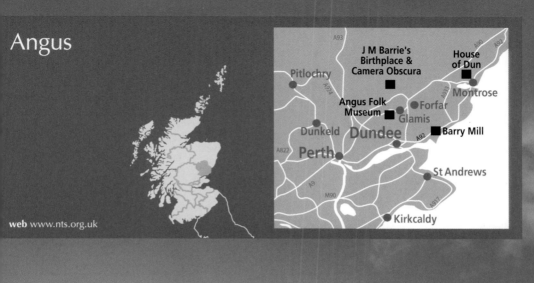

web www.nts.org.uk

J M Barrie's Birthplace & Camera Obscura

House of Dun

Pitlochry

Montrose

Angus Folk Museum

Forfar

Glamis

Dunkeld

Dundee

Barry Mill

Perth

St Andrews

Kirkcaldy

Angus Folk Museum

Kirkwynd, Glamis, Forfar, Angus DD8 1RT

tel 0844 493 2141

Experience life as a Scottish landworker at this fascinating folk museum. Housed in six 18th-century Angus cottages, the collection offers a vivid insight into the realities of rural life over the past 200 years

The *Life on the Land* exhibition, based around a reconstructed farm courtyard, houses the bothy, smiddy, stables and the hearse house. Here you can see the beautifully restored 'Glenisla' horse-drawn hearse.

E **£** D

OS Ref: NO385468
Road: Off A94, in Glamis, 5m SW of Forfar **Bus:** Limited service from Dundee, Forfar and Kirriemuir; Meffan Coaches (01575) 572130 or Strathtay Buses (01382) 227201

Baby changing facilities, pushchairs allowed in museum, baby backpacks allowed, storage for pushchairs

Explanatory text: French, German, Italian, Spanish

Parking at museum. All main rooms. Toilet. Wheelchair available

P Small car park adjacent to cottages. Coach and further car parking in village, 200 metres

A Collection brought together by Jean, Lady Maitland, and presented by the local trustees. The Earl of Strathmore and Kinghorne donated the steading in 1957 and the hearse house in 1983

Museum			M . . . . S S
	23 Mar to 30 Jun	11.30-4.30	M . . . . S S
	1 Jul to 31 Aug	10.30-4.30	M . . T F S S
	1 Sep to 28 Oct	11.30-4.30	M . . . . S S

Barry Mill

Barry, Carnoustie, Angus DD7 7RJ

tel 0844 493 2140

Now a haven of tranquillity, in the 19th century Barry Mill was alive with the splash of the water-wheel, the rumble of machinery and the smell of grinding corn. The mill was at the heart of this small rural community, providing work and social opportunities for local people. Until as late as 1982 the mill was still at work – the last of its kind in Angus – producing oatmeal and finally animal feed.

Now one of Scotland's last working water-powered corn mills and an A listed building, it's a magnificent example of the country's industrial heritage and you can learn all about the working of the mill from a real miller. The machinery freewheels daily and a live demonstration of this disappearing craft is normally held on Sundays and for pre-booked parties.

E **→** **🚻** **🏕** **P** **£** D

OS Ref: NO534349
Road: N of Barry village between A92 and A930, 2m W of Carnoustie **Cycle:** 1m from NCN 1 **Bus:** Strathtay Buses from Dundee, Carnoustie and Arbroath stop in Barry village (½m); (01382) 228054 **Rail:** Carnoustie station 2m

Baby changing facilities, pushchairs ground/lower ground floors only, storage for pushchairs

! Dogs are welcome but must be kept under control at all times

Can alight at mill by arrangement. Ground floor, single step to lower ground floor. Toilet. Grass paths

A Purchased in 1988

Grounds and Lade-side walk	All year		Until dusk	M T W T F S S
Mill		23 Mar to 31 Oct	12-5 (Sun 1-5)	M . . T F S S

J M Barrie's Birthplace

9 Brechin Road, Kirriemuir, Angus DD8 4BX

tel 0844 493 2142

The magical story of Peter Pan's adventures has captivated children for over a century. His creator, J M Barrie, was born here in 1860, one of ten children. See how his early life at Kirriemuir with his brothers and sisters inspired the characters and storylines in his work. The wash house here became his first theatre – could it also have inspired the Wendy House in *Peter Pan*? Tread carefully in the garden – there's a living-willow crocodile! The house next door, No 11, holds a fascinating exhibition about Barrie's life and his literary and theatrical works, along with important memorabilia such as theatrical costumes and an original manuscript of *Peter Pan* with Barrie's own notations.

E 🏕 🏛 **£** D

OS Ref: NO387540
Road: A90/A926, in Kirriemuir, 6m NW of Forfar **Bus:** Strathtay Buses (No 20) from Dundee via Forfar; (01382) 228054

Pushchairs ground floor/garden only, baby backpacks allowed, storage for pushchairs. Children's play area, children's activities

Explanatory text: Dutch, French, Gaelic, German, Italian, Japanese, Spanish, Swedish

Museum, wash house, garden. Step (18cm) to reception room and tearoom (ramp available). Stairlift to 1st floor. Toilets 100 metres

Braille information sheets

Induction loop in exhibition room

P   Local authority car park 200 metres

A   Given in 1937 by Mr D Alves, with additional funds for restoration

Birthplace				
23 Mar to 30 Jun	12-5		M T W . . S S
1 Jul to 31 Aug	11-5		M T W T F S S
1 Sep to 28 Oct	12-5		M T W . . S S

Kirriemuir Camera Obscura

Kirrie Hill, Kirriemuir, Angus DD8 4PT

tel 0844 493 2142

Step into the darkened interior of the camera obscura on Kirrie Hill and you'll be amazed by the striking views of the surrounding countryside. How does it work? Our guide will be happy to explain. There are only three of these fascinating installations still remaining in Scotland. This one was given to the community of Kirriemuir by J M Barrie, the creator of *Peter Pan*, after he was honoured with the freedom of the town in 1930.

Please be aware that at times the camera obscura may be closed due to weather conditions. Please check with Barrie's Birthplace if in doubt.

➜ 🏕 P **£** E

OS Ref: NO388546
Road: A90/A926, in Kirriemuir, 6m NW of Forfar. Signposted from Kirriemuir High Street **Bus:** Strathtay Buses (No 20) from Dundee via Forfar; (01382) 228054

Pushchairs ground floor/garden only, baby backpacks allowed, storage for pushchairs. Children's adventure playground

Explanatory text: French, Italian

Interpretation on ground floor, but camera inaccessible. Public toilet 100 metres

15 steps to camera

A   Managed by the Trust since 1999

Camera Obscura			
23 Mar to 30 Jun	12-5 (Sun 1-5)		. . . . . S S
1 Jul to 30 Sep	12-5 (Sun 1-5)		M T W T F S S

Last viewing 4.40. Also open Bank Holiday Mondays.

With so much history behind it, the rich character of the House of Dun is sure to keep you occupied all day. The Dun Estate was home to the Erskine family from 1375 until 1980, but archaeological evidence shows that people have lived here for at least 9,000 years.

The handsome Georgian house overlooking the Montrose Basin was completed in 1730 by William Adam for David Erskine, the 13th Laird of Dun. Inside, grand public rooms with elaborate plasterwork sit alongside family apartments. Here you'll discover collections of 18th- and 19th-century furniture, porcelain and portraits, along with exquisite embroidery by the most famous lady of the house – Lady Augusta FitzClarence, daughter of William IV and the actress Dorothy Jordan. Be entertained by the model theatre display with its scaled-down stage and cast of miniature costumed characters. And visit the courtyard buildings where you'll find a handloom weaving workshop and a second-hand bookshop. Our 'Crafts of Angus Showcase' shop sells a wide variety of locally produced crafts.

The house sits in its own formal gardens with parkland and woodland beyond. You're free to explore and enjoy the Victorian walled garden and wooded den before venturing further afield to the Montrose Basin Local Nature Reserve. The Trust owns much of the western half, and it is internationally important for its migratory wading birds and wildfowl. Down at the River South Esk there are salmon and sea trout. The Trust owns fishing rights, and you can buy permits by contacting the property.

We've recently introduced two outstanding collections to the Library: the Hutchison Collection of 20th-century paintings by prominent Scottish Colourists and the Stirling Collection, an eclectic variety of objects – from 18th-century Regency furniture to more quirky items from the 1960s.

£ C

OS Ref: NO670598
Road: On A935, 3m W of Montrose **Cycle:** 3m from NCN 1 **Bus:** Strathtay Buses; (01382) 228054 **Rail:** Montrose station, 3m

Guided tours only except on last Sunday of each month. First tour 11.10 (high season), 12.15 (low season)

Tearoom

Baby changing facilities, storage for pushchairs, pushchairs in garden only, adventure playground, children's quiz, regular children's events

Salmon fishing season Feb to Oct. Please contact property for further details. Occasionally parts or all of the property may be closed during normal opening hours due to functions, particularly on Saturdays – please call the property before you visit

Civil wedding licence, exclusive dinners, private parties & receptions

Explanatory text: French, German

Four disabled parking bays in courtyard. Basement and ground floor rooms (via stairlift), no access to 1st floor. Tearoom, shop. East walled garden and terrace. Toilet. Wheelchair available. Level access by farm track to Montrose Basin Nature Reserve, with grass path to bird hide

Shallow steps to 1st floor

Guided tours. Braille and large print information sheets

Subtitled video in basement

House, tenanted estate and woodland (368ha) bequeathed in 1980 by Mrs M A A Lovett

Garden and Estate	All year	9 until dusk	M	T	W	T	F	S	S
House	23 Mar to 30 Jun	12-5	.	.	W	T	F	S	S
	1 Jul to 31 Aug	11-5	M	T	W	T	F	S	S
	1 Sep to 28 Oct	12-5	.	.	W	T	F	S	S

Last admission 45 mins before closing.
House also open on Bank Holiday weekends from Friday to Monday inclusive.

Aberdeen & Grampian

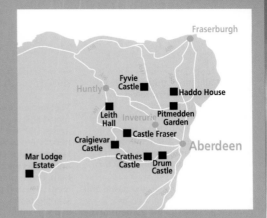

Fraserburgh

Huntly

Fyvie Castle

Haddo House

Leith Hall

Inverurie

Pitmedden Garden

Craigievar Castle

Castle Fraser

Mar Lodge Estate

Crathes Castle

Drum Castle

Aberdeen

web www.nts.org.uk

Castle Fraser, Garden & Estate

Sauchen, Inverurie, Aberdeenshire AB51 7LD

tel 0844 493 2164
fax 0844 493 2165

ranger service
tel 0844 493 2167

Approaching Castle Fraser down the Broad Walk, the granite walls rising up to the distinctive turrets make an imposing sight. This was the impression the lairds intended as the present castle took shape between 1575 and 1636 – a statement of pride for the Fraser family and a show of strength to any would-be detractors.

As you venture through the castle and up to the round tower, with its panoramic views of the gardens and estate beyond, you get a sense of life from the medieval to the Victorian period. One of the most evocative rooms is the strikingly simple Great Hall. Meanwhile, in the traditional Victorian kitchen, you can enjoy home baking, tasty soups and sandwiches.

The castle contains many Fraser family portraits, including one by Raeburn, and fine 19th-century carpets, curtains and bed hangings. There are other quirky features for you to discover – such as the Laird's Lug, hidden trapdoors revealing secret stairs, a spy hole, a room full of stuffed animals and a wooden leg!

The gardens have recently undergone major redevelopment. The pathways in the 18th-century walled garden have been reinstated, and new lawns laid around island borders containing unusual as well as more traditional herbaceous plants. There's also a new medicinal and culinary border with scented plants, and an organic fruit and vegetable garden.

Children will love the 'Woodland Secrets' area, where they can play safely amongst wooden sculptures, a bamboo snake, musical instruments, tepees, a tree house and a stone circle. 'Words in the Woods' is a grassed amphitheatre used as a meeting place and venue for poetry reading and storytelling. Elsewhere, the estate contains an artificial lake, mixed woodland and open farmland, with two waymarked walks giving magnificent views of the local hills.

£ C

OS Ref: NJ722125
Road: Off A944, 4m N of Dunecht and 16m W of Aberdeen **Bus:** Stagecoach Bluebird from Aberdeen bus station; (01224) 212266

Leaflet available

Tearoom

Baby changing facilities, baby carriers available, storage for pushchairs, pushchairs ground floor/garden only, baby backpacks not allowed, adventure playground, children's activities

Civil wedding licence, exclusive dinners, private parties, receptions & marquee areas

Explanatory text: Chinese, Doric, Dutch, Polish, French, German, Italian, Japanese, Russian, Spanish, Swedish

Parking at castle. Entrance hall, tearoom and shop (ramp) only. Toilet. Walled garden accessible

Printed room guides

Scented walled garden. Large print guide

A Castle and 10.5ha of ground given with an endowment by Major & Mrs Michael Smiley in 1976. A further 127ha of surrounding land purchased in 1993

			M T W T F S S
Garden and Grounds	All year		M T W T F S S
Castle, Tearoom	27 Mar to 30 Jun	12-5 (last entry 4.15)	. . W T F S S
and Shop	1 Jul to 31 Aug	11-5 (last entry 4.15)	M T W T F S S
	1 Sep to 31 Oct	12-5 (last entry 4.15)	. . W T F S S
Restaurant	All year	Evenings only	. . . T F S S

Bookings only, please call 01467 642834

Property also open on Bank Holiday Mondays.

Craigievar Castle
Alford, Aberdeenshire AB33 8JF

tel 0844 493 2174
fax 0844 493 2163
ranger service
tel 0844 493 2167

Craigievar's great tower has changed very little since it was altered and completed by Master William Forbes in the early 17th century, after he had bought it from the Mortimer family. The Forbes family (later Forbes-Sempill) continued to live in the castle for the next 350 years and when a group of benefactors (including members of the family) bought the castle and presented it to the National Trust for Scotland, it came complete with the vast majority of the contents, collected and lovingly preserved over the centuries by the family. First and foremost, Craigievar was a home and it is the special family atmosphere that endears it to so many visitors and which the Trust has tried to preserve.

Surrounding the castle are extensive parkland grounds. There is also a small Victorian kitchen garden and a Scottish glen garden. Additionally there are two waymarked walks. The first loop of the trail that runs below the castle is fairly easy walking through open woodland, which seems to glow blue in the early summer when the bluebells are in flower. The rest of this trail leads through woods, marsh and farmland with beautiful views of the castle and surrounding hills, although there are very steep sections.

The second trail, which is longer and some parts are much rougher in character, winds through the extensive woodland above the castle. Again it affords wonderful views over the surrounding countryside. The final section of this trail shares the main drive and visitors are advised to beware of traffic, especially if accompanied by young children or dogs.

£ B

OS Ref: NJ566095
Road: On A980, 6m S of Alford, 15m N of Banchory and 26m W of Aberdeen

Guided tours only. Small coach parties by prior arrangement (max 24 people)

Baby backpacks not allowed, storage for pushchairs. Pushchairs allowed in grounds only, children's events/tours

Dogs welcome, but must be kept under control at all times. The outside toilets close at the end of Oct

Dutch, French, German, Italian, Spanish

Parking at castle. Access to castle difficult. Grounds accessible

Many steep spiral stairs

Touch tours (book in advance). Large-print information sheet

Castle and 13ha of ground bought from the Forbes-Sempill family by a consortium of benefactors and presented to the Trust in 1963. An additional 24ha of farmland purchased in 1978 providing a safeguard for its amenity. Following an appeal, a further 84.3ha of woodland purchased in 2004 to protect amenity

Grounds	All year	11-5.30	**M**	**T**	**W**	**T**	**F**	**S**	**S**
Castle	30 Mar to 30 Jun	11-4.45 (last entry)	**M**	**T**	.	.	**F**	**S**	**S**
	1 Jul to 31 Aug	11-4.45 (last entry)	**M**	**T**	**W**	**T**	**F**	**S**	**S**
	1 Sep to 30 Sep	11-4.45 (last entry)	**M**	**T**	.	.	**F**	**S**	**S**

Guided tours only. Numbers on guided tours are limited and at peak times visitors may have to wait for the next available tour.
Tours can be booked in advance by calling the property.

Crathes Castle, Garden & Estate

Standing against a background
of rolling hills and set in its own
glorious gardens, this magical
turreted castle is a favourite
destination for fans of Scottish
history, gardeners and romantics.

Crathes Castle, Garden & Estate

Banchory, Aberdeenshire AB31 5QJ

tel 0844 493 2166
fax 0844 493 2169

ranger service
tel 0844 493 2167
shop tel 0844 493 2168

Crathes is a magnificent 16th-century tower house standing on an estate granted to the Burnett family in 1323 by King Robert the Bruce. He presented them with the ancient Horn of Leys, which you can see today in the Great Hall. The horn symbol was added to the family coat-of-arms and you'll see it throughout the castle – on the painted ceilings and carved onto the laird's bed.

Watch out for the 'trip' step, intended to disconcert attackers climbing the staircase. Imagine being a member of court walking up and down the extravagant long gallery, or picture Lady Katherine and her friends playing music, sewing and chatting in the Muses Room. Feel a slight chill? It could be the Green Lady, Crathes' own ghost who is said to have first appeared in the mid-18th century. The walled garden is really eight gardens, ranging from the formal to the modern. The massive yew hedges were planted as early as 1702, while the Golden Garden was introduced by the Trust in 1973. Most famous of all are the June Borders, two lavish beds of herbaceous colour with the castle itself as a backdrop.

Follow one of the waymarked trails out into the surrounding countryside. There are woodland, farmland and freshwater habitats where you may see roe deer, red squirrels, woodpeckers, buzzards, kingfishers and herons. And if you're very lucky you may catch a glimpse of an otter or red kite.

OS Ref: NO735967
Road: On A93, 15m W of Aberdeen and 3m E of Banchory
Bus: Stagecoach Bluebird (No 201) from Aberdeen bus station stops at estate entrance; (01224) 212266
Rail: Aberdeen station, 15m
Airport: Aberdeen (Dyce), 12m

Courtyard café

Baby changing facilities, baby backpacks not allowed in the castle, storage for pushchairs, play areas, adventure play area, children's quiz, trail, dressing-up costumes for educational tours

Civil wedding licence, exclusive dinners, private parties, receptions & marquee areas

Guidebook: French, German. Explanatory text: Azerbaijani, Czech, Danish, Dutch, French, German, Hebrew, Italian, Japanese, Norwegian, Polish, Portuguese, Russian, Spanish, Swedish

Parking adjacent to Horsemill bookshop. Ground floor of castle, part of garden and grounds, viewpoint trail. Shop, restaurants, occasional exhibitions (entrance to upper floor from disabled car park area – see staff to open door). Toilets. Wheelchairs available

Gifted in 1951 with an endowment by Sir James Burnett of Leys, Bt

			M	T	W	T	F	S	S
Garden and Estate*	All year	9-sunset	M	T	W	T	F	S	S
Castle	5 Jan to 22 Mar	10.30-3.45	.	.	.	.	.	S	S
	23 Mar to 31 Oct	10.30-4.45	M	T	W	T	F	S	S
	1 Nov to 23 Dec**	10.30-3.45	.	.	.	.	.	S	S
Shop	3 Jan to 31 Mar	10-4	.	T	W	T	F	S	S
	1 Apr to 31 Oct	10-5	M	T	W	T	F	S	S
	1 Nov to 23 Dec**	10-4	.	T	W	T	F	S	S
Courtyard Café	3 Jan to 31 Mar	10-4	.	T	W	T	F	S	S
	1 Apr to 31 Oct	9.30-5	M	T	W	T	F	S	S
	1 Nov to 23 Dec**	10-4	.	T	W	T	F	S	S

Last admission to castle 45 mins before closing.
*Estate closed 24-26 Dec and 1-2 Jan. Garden will be closed for an event on first weekend in July
** Castle, shop and courtyard café open daily 27-31 Dec

Drum Castle, Garden & Estate

Drumoak, by Banchory, Aberdeenshire AB31 5EY

tel 0844 493 2161
fax 0844 493 2162

ranger service
tel 0844 493 2167

A visit to Drum is a little like striding across the centuries. The castle building and estate lands were given in 1323 by King Robert the Bruce to William de Irwyn as a reward for 20 years of loyal service. The castle has evolved with the additions made to the building over the years. Here you'll find a medieval tower, a Jacobean mansion house and several 'modern' additions by Victorian lairds. This was the work of 24 generations of the Irvine family who lived here for over 650 years.

Imagine what life must have been like in the High Hall, still in its medieval state with unglazed windows, bare stone walls and earth floor. Climb the ladder to the battlements and take in the amazing views of the surrounding countryside.

In contrast to the tower, the Garden of Historic Roses is a remarkably peaceful corner. Here you can see roses from the shores of Japan, rugged yet delicately perfumed, and roses from China bringing peach and orange to a colour palette of reds, pinks and whites. Feast your eyes on the curtains of roses cascading down the centuries-old walls, heavy with scent and reverberating with buzzing bumblebees. Don't miss the 20th-century pond garden, pinetum and holly collection, as well as the Old Wood of Drum. This remnant of the ancient Royal Forest and Park of Drum is now a Site of Special Scientific Interest, where you may spot woodpeckers, wrens, red squirrels and roe deer among the old oaks.

2013 Entry to Drum Castle, Garden & Estate is reduced because the 13th-century tower and library are closed for essential conservation work. However, the rest of the 17th-century Jacobean castle and chapel are open to visitors, and the exquisite Garden of Historic Roses and Old Wood of Drum Trail make the estate a must-see attraction.

OS Ref: NJ796005
Road: Off A93, 3m W of Peterculter, 10m W of Aberdeen and 8m E of Banchory **Bus:** Stagecoach Bluebird (No 201) from Aberdeen bus station; (01224) 212266. Bus stops at road end, ½m walk to castle **Rail:** Aberdeen station, 10m **Airport:** Aberdeen (Dyce), 8m

Tearoom

Baby changing facilities, storage for pushchairs, baby hip carriers available, play areas, adventure play area, regular children's events, children's quiz/trail

Civil wedding licence, exclusive dinners, private parties, receptions

Explanatory text: French, Dutch, German, Italian, Japanese, Norwegian, Russian, Spanish, Swedish

Parking at castle and Historic Rose Garden. Access with assistance to ground floor of castle (one step), Pond Garden, Historic Rose Garden, tearoom, shop. Toilet. Wheelchair available

Braille information sheets. Large-print information. Scented rose garden. Touch tours (book in advance)

Bequeathed with an endowment by Mr H Q Forbes Irvine of Drum in 1976

			M T W T F S S
Grounds	All year		M T W T F S S
Castle, Tearoom	29 Mar to 30 Jun	11-4 (last entry)	M . . T F S S
and Shop	1 Jul to 31 Aug	11-4 (last entry)	M T W T F S S
	1 Sep to 29 Sep	11-4 (last entry)	M . . T F S S
Garden of Historic Roses	29 Mar to 31 Oct	11-4.15 (last entry)	M T W T F S S

Fyvie Castle, Garden & Estate

Fyvie, Turriff, Aberdeenshire AB53 8JS

tel 0844 493 2182
fax 0844 493 2181
ranger service
tel 0844 493 2167

Ghosts, legends and folklore are all woven into the tapestry of Fyvie's 800-year history. Each tower of this magnificent Scottish Baronial fortress is traditionally associated with one of the castle's five successive families – Preston, Meldrum, Seton, Gordon and Forbes-Leith. You can see their influences today among the medieval stones and the lavish Edwardian interiors, and imagine what castle life must have been like for the families and their royal guests – among them Robert the Bruce and Charles I.

Art lovers will appreciate Fyvie's rich portrait collection, including works by Batoni, Romney, Gainsborough, Opie, Lawrence and Hoppner. The castle also boasts one of the largest private collections of Raeburns in the world. There's an equally impressive collection of fine furniture, tapestries, arms and armour throughout the castle's vast chambers, and a great stone wheel staircase – the finest of its kind in Scotland.

Save time for a leisurely stroll around Fyvie's grounds and lochside, landscaped in the early 19th century. The 18th-century walled garden has recently been redeveloped as a garden of Scottish fruits and vegetables, and this, along with the American Garden and other parkland areas, is open all year.

OS Ref: NJ764393
Road: Off A947, 8m SE of Turriff and 25m NW of Aberdeen
Bus: Stagecoach Bluebird from Aberdeen bus station to Fyvie village, 1m; (01224) 212266

Tearoom

Baby changing facilities, pushchairs can be stored in Front Hall

Civil wedding licence, exclusive dinners, private parties, receptions & marquee areas

Guidebook: French, German. Explanatory text: Dutch, French, German, Italian, Norwegian, Spanish

Parking in front of castle. Front Hall only. Walled garden, American garden. Tearoom. Toilet

Steps to various rooms

Braille information sheets. Herbs and scented planting in walled garden

Castle and grounds purchased in 1984

Garden	All year	9-sunset	M	T	W	T	F	S	S
Grounds	All year		M	T	W	T	F	S	S
Castle, Shop	29 Mar to 30 Jun	12-5	M	T	W	.	.	S	S
and Tearoom	1 Jul to 31 Aug	11-5	M	T	W	T	F	S	S
	1 Sep to 31 Oct	12-5	M	T	W	.	.	S	S

Last admission to castle 4.15pm.
Property open on Bank Holiday weekends from Friday to Monday inclusive.

Haddo House

Methlick, Ellon, Aberdeenshire AB41 7EQ

tel 0844 493 2179

A visit to Haddo is sure to keep you occupied all day, there's so much to see and do. For all its grandeur, visitors to the house often remark how homely it feels. Perhaps this has something to do with the fact that the Gordon family have lived at Haddo continuously for over 400 years. Originally designed by William Adam in 1732 and refurbished in 1880, the present house combines crisp Georgian architecture with sumptuous late Victorian interiors. Throughout the house and grounds, family portraits, sculptures and memorabilia build up a fascinating history of the Gordon family over the centuries. The superb collection of portraits includes a painting of George, Lord Haddo by Pompeo Batoni, and works by William Mosman, Sir Thomas Lawrence and the 'Castles of Aberdeenshire' series by James Giles.

Visit the old stables and you'll find our shop, which sells an excellent range of gifts, then call into the period tearoom to sample some delicious home baking.

Don't leave without visiting the delightful terrace garden with geometric flower beds and fountain, a lavish herbaceous border and a collection of commemorative trees. A magnificent avenue of lime trees leads to adjacent Haddo Country Park with its lakes, monuments, walks and wildlife.

OS Ref: NJ868347
Road: Off B999 near Tarves, at 'Raxton' crossroads, 19m N of Aberdeen, 4m N of Pitmedden and 10m NW of Ellon **Cycle:** 1m from NCN 1 **Bus:** Stagecoach Bluebird from Aberdeen bus station; (01224) 212266. Buses stop in Tarves, c4m walk.

E During Easter school holidays there will be children's tours, family events and special interest tours in the house. See website for details

Guided tours only

Tearoom

Storage for pushchairs in Front Hall, children's quiz

Civil wedding licence, exclusive dinners, private parties, receptions & marquee areas

Information sheets: German, French, Italian, Spanish

Disabled visitors may alight at front door, parking nearby. House (lift to 1st floor), part of garden, Country Park, shop, restaurant. Toilets. Wheelchair available

P Aberdeenshire Council, Pay & Display

A Haddo House, its gardens, hall and stable block, and 7.7ha of the policies acquired by the Secretary of State for Scotland in 1978, through National Land Fund procedures, at the wish of the 4th Marquess of Aberdeen and Temair who also provided an endowment. The house and garden were opened by the Trust in 1979. The adjacent Country Park is run by Aberdeenshire Council

			M	T	W	T	F	S	S
Garden and Grounds	All year	9-sunset	M	T	W	T	F	S	S
House*	29 Mar to 30 Jun		M	.	.	.	F	S	S
	1 Jul to 31 Aug		M	T	W	T	F	S	S
	1 Sep to 27 Oct		M	.	.	.	F	S	S
Shop	29 Mar to 27 Oct	11-4.30	M	T	W	T	F	S	S
	28 Oct to 6 Apr 2014	12-4	.	.	.	.	.	S	S
Tearoom	29 Mar to 14 Apr	11-5	M	T	W	T	F	S	S
	15 Apr to 31 May	11-5	M	.	.	.	F	S	S
	1 Jun to 31 Aug	11-5	M	T	W	T	F	S	S
	1 Sep to 27 Oct	11-5	M	.	.	.	F	S	S
	28 Oct to 6 Apr 2014	11-4	.	.	.	.	.	S	S

** Haddo House is open for guided tours only, at 11.30am, 1.30pm and 3.30pm. **Pre-booking is recommended** – call property, book in person at the shop or email haddo@nts.org.uk. Please note that the house may be closed occasionally for functions and it is advisable to phone before visiting. Last orders in tearoom 30 mins before closing.*

Leith Hall Garden & Estate

Huntly, Aberdeenshire AB54 4NQ

Leith Hall was built over three centuries, starting in 1650, and remained the home of the Leith-Hay family until the mid-20th century. Along with the house, all the furnishings and paintings were left to the Trust by the family.

Today, it's a picturesque and tranquil place – but it has been touched by tragedy in the past. The last two lairds died within months of each other in 1939. And in 1763 John Leith was murdered in Aberdeen. His ghost reputedly still walks the hallways and the story has been featured on the TV programme *Most Haunted*.

The beautiful gardens here are one of the Trust's hidden gems. From the top of the garden there are spectacular views of Aberdeenshire and the surrounding hills. At 186m above sea level it is the highest altitude garden in our care and boasts a coldest recorded temperature of -28°C! But the south-facing slope of the garden makes it an ideal location for many plants from all over the world to thrive.

The remarkable herbaceous and catmint borders that run either side of the zigzag path are one of the longest of their kind in Scotland, at nearly 100m. Other features include the rock garden, vegetable garden and the Moon Gate – a rare focal point along the wall of the east garden.

The wider estate offers three waymarked trails. The all access trail around the pond leads you through mixed woodland and is home to various wildfowl, grey herons and even the occasional otter. If you have more time you could follow the Kirkhill trail through farmland and mixed woodland, with the option of visiting the old kirkyard, resting place of the Leith-Hay family. The slightly more demanding Craigfall trail will take you up the hill, through a small alder wood, and on up to a viewpoint overlooking the surrounding countryside and Leith Hall itself.

New for 2013 Cadbury Easter Egg Trail. The Hall is due to re-open to the public in summer. See website for further details.

OS Ref: NJ541298
Road: On B9002, 1m W of Kennethmont and 34m NW of Aberdeen **Bus**: No 306 from Huntly **Rail**: Huntly or Insch stations, both 7m

The Hall is available for weddings, corporate entertaining, pre-booked tours and other events. School groups are also welcome

Sloping walled garden: parking at top on left near Gardener's cottage, path to viewpoint. Pond walk accessible with assistance

Scented walled garden

Given in 1945 by the Hon Mrs Leith-Hay

Garden	All year	9-sunset	M T W T F S S
Grounds	All year	9-sunset	M T W T F S S
Hall	Please see www.nts.org.uk for up-to-date information		

Mar Lodge Estate

Estate Office, Mar Lodge, Braemar,
Aberdeenshire AB35 5YJ

tel 0844 493 2172
fax 0844 493 2171

ranger service tel 0844 493 2173
lodge housekeeper
tel 0844 493 2170

Striding across the wild open spaces of Mar Lodge Estate you'll experience a unique sense of freedom. Located in the heart of the Cairngorms National Park, the 29,380ha (72,598a) estate takes in 15 Munros (mountains over 3,000ft), including four of the five highest mountains in the UK. Walkers can choose from a wide range of routes – from low-lying woodland and riverside walks, to the high tops and long-distance walks such as the Lairig Ghru leading to Speyside. The main access point is the Linn of Dee car park, with nearby walks offering stunning views of a scenic gorge. During the summer months the ranger service offers a variety of guided walks to suit all abilities.

The estate is recognised as one of the most important nature conservation landscapes in the British Isles. Part of the estate lies within the Cairngorms National Nature Reserve, and a number of sites have been designated Sites of Special Scientific Interest. Wildlife enthusiasts may observe pine martens, red deer, red squirrels and, most majestic of all, the golden eagle.

The estate also contains one of the country's largest areas of Scheduled Ancient Monuments – from post-medieval townships to remnants of early 19th-century sheep farming and of the later 19th-century sporting estate. These nationally important remains give a fascinating insight into the life and culture which existed at a turning point in the history of these glens. The estate also has some fine examples of Victorian architecture, which demonstrate the influence of the Victorians on Deeside and their eagerness to holiday in the Highlands.

Long-term conservation is a priority at Mar Lodge Estate, in particular the regeneration of native Caledonian pinewoods by reducing the damage caused by grazing red deer. Elsewhere you'll see evidence of the Trust's valuable work repairing and maintaining footpaths, and mitigating the effects of vehicle tracks.

Shooting, stalking and fishing are all available here, and the management of the estate provides a balance between sport and conservation. Visitors can learn more about this during their visit. The estate also provides accommodation, and the Lodge is becoming increasingly popular as a venue for weddings, conferences and seminars.

OS Ref: NO096899
Road: 3m W of Braemar. Access from A93 via unclassified road to Linn of Dee **Bus:** Stagecoach Bluebird (No 201), Aberdeen to Braemar; (01224) 212266. No public transport from Braemar to estate.
Rail: Aberdeen station, 65m

Groups by prior arrangement. Facilities for groups of disabled visitors. Contact the estate for details

Programme of guided walks and events during summer months. Contact ranger service for advice on visiting wider estate – walking routes, wild camping, access

Opportunities for walks for all abilities

Please keep dogs under control or on leads, especially during bird nesting season, Apr-Jul. Mar Lodge booklet available on receipt of SAE, Mar Lodge Woods and People available by post on receipt of £2.50

Civil wedding licence, exclusive dinners, private parties, receptions & marquee areas

Self-catering accommodation for up to 61 guests available in luxurious apartments within the Lodge, two sumptuous secluded country houses and the bunkhouse-style basecamp

Parking and toilet at Linn of Dee car park. Area immediately surrounding Lodge has level tarmac surface but wider estate has rough country paths

Linn of Dee, 6m W of Braemar, Pay and Display

Purchased in 1995

Estate	All year		**M T W T F S S**

Scotland's National Nature Reserves

OPEN DAYS at Lodge for non-residents on Easter Sunday and first Sunday of September, 10-4.

Pitmedden Garden

Ellon, Aberdeenshire AB41 7PD

tel 0844 493 2177
fax 0844 493 2178
ranger service
tel 0844 493 2167

It's hard to imagine a garden today being planted on such an extravagant scale. The heart of the property is the formal walled garden originally laid out in 1675 by Sir Alexander Seton. In the 1950s, the Trust set about re-creating the gardens following designs dating from the 17th century. Today, Pitmedden features over 5 miles of box hedging arranged in intricate patterns to form six parterres. These parterres are filled with some 40,000 plants bursting with colour in the summer months.

Extensive herbaceous borders provide an abundance of colour and texture throughout the season. Two new borders were added in 2004. Honeysuckle, jasmine and roses create a succession of fragrances, while fountains, topiary, sundials and a fascinating herb garden add to the sense of discovery around the walled garden. If you're a keen gardener, Pitmedden is a great source of inspiration and ideas.

Over 80 varieties of apple trees adorn the high granite walls, offering a spectacular show of blossom and scent in spring. On the last Sunday in September we hold harvest celebrations with musical entertainment, and you can buy fruits harvested from the gardens.

The adjacent Museum of Farming Life boasts an extensive collection of domestic and agricultural artefacts of a bygone era. For the more adventurous, the woodland walk extends for a mile and a half round the estate and takes in ponds, rhododendrons, a lime kiln and a nature hut with information about the wider estate. The picnic area is an ideal spot to stop for lunch, and you can even enjoy a game of boules on our own pétanque piste.

OS Ref: NJ884280
Road: On A920, 1m W of Pitmedden village and 14m N of Aberdeen
Cycle: 2m from NCN 1
Bus: Infrequent service passes road end; Stagecoach Bluebird (01224) 212266

Tearoom

Baby changing facilities, children's quizzes

Explanatory text: Danish, Dutch, French, German, Italian, Spanish

Parking. Visitor Centre, tearoom. Upper garden and parts of museum accessible. Lower parterres accessible via alternative entrance – ask staff. Toilet. Wheelchairs available

Scented plants

A Given with an endowment by Major James Keith in 1952. Collection of the Museum of Farming Life given by the Trustees of William Cook of Little Meldrum, Tarves in 1978, together with a pecuniary legacy

			M T W T F S S
Grounds	All year		M T W T F S S
Garden, Museum of Farming Life and Shop	1 May to 30 Sep	10-5.30 (last entry 5pm)	M T W T F S S
Tearoom	1 May to 30 Sep	10.30-4.30	M T W T F S S

Lochaber

Skye

Glenfinnan Monument

Fort William

A830

A87

A82

A86

A861

Glencoe & Dalness

A82

A849

Craignure

Mull

Oban

A85

Crianlarich

web www.nts.org.uk

Glenfinnan Monumen

Glenfinnan Monument

Visitor Centre, Glenfinnan, Highland PH37 4LT

tel/fax 0844 493 2221

On 19 August 1745, at the head of Loch Shiel, Prince Charles Edward Stuart raised his Standard, marking the start of his campaign to restore the exiled Stuarts to the throne. From this spot, Bonnie Prince Charlie and his followers made it as far south as Derby before their eventual defeat the following year at Culloden. The Glenfinnan Monument was designed by the Scottish architect James Gillespie Graham, and was erected in 1815 by Alexander Macdonald of Glenaladale as a tribute to the clansmen who fought and died in the cause of the Stuarts. You can find out more about Bonnie Prince Charlie's campaign at the Visitor Centre. Fans of Harry Potter, meanwhile, might recognise the viaduct nearby that features in the movies.

$£^E$

OS Ref: NM906805
Road: A830, 18½m W of Fort William
Rail: Glenfinnan station, 1m

Baby changing facilities, baby backpacks allowed, storage for pushchairs

Audio programme: Dutch, French, Gaelic, German, Spanish

Parking at Visitor Centre. Exhibition, snack-bar, shop. Toilet. Wheelchair available

Narrow steep steps in monument

Induction loop in Visitor Centre

A Presented to the Trust in 1938 by Sir Walter Blount, proprietor, on behalf of himself, the Trustees of Glenaladale Estates and the Roman Catholic Diocese of Argyll and the Isles. A conservation agreement protecting 11ha surrounding the monument was made by Mr A MacKellaig

Site	All year			**M**	**T**	**W**	**T**	**F**	**S S**
Visitor Centre, Shop and Snack-Bar	23 Mar to 31 Oct	10-5		**M**	**T**	**W**	**T**	**F**	**S S**

Last tickets for Monument 15 mins before closing.

Glencoe & Dalness

In every sense a dramatic landscape. The peaks of Glencoe stand as a monument to one of the most tragic events in Scotland's history.

Glencoe & Dalness

Visitor Centre, Glencoe, Argyll PH49 4HX

tel 0844 493 2222
fax 0844 493 2223

With towering mountains sweeping down on both sides, Glencoe is at once spectacularly beautiful and yet strangely forbidding – a legacy perhaps of the infamous massacre that took place here on a snow-driven February night in 1692. Today, visitors are drawn to Glencoe for its dramatic landscape, wealth of wildlife and varied geology. Glencoe is also the cradle of Scottish mountaineering and the area provides some of the finest climbing and walking country in the Highlands.

Nestling into the landscape at the foot of the glen is the award-winning eco-friendly Glencoe Visitor Centre. A perfect stopping-off point if you're travelling through on the A82, with a café, a well-stocked shop and a viewing platform. Here you can access the information point and get weather forecasts, as well as friendly advice from rangers at the outlook station.

Learn more about the area with a visit to the exhibition *Living on The Edge*, which has exciting interactive displays and activities for adults and children. Find out what it feels like to climb on ice, discover how the glen was formed, and try your hand at solving the conservation issues faced by the Trust.

During the summer, a programme of ranger-led walks and events start from the Visitor Centre. Our popular Wildlife Land Rover Safaris allow visitors of all abilities to get a completely different view of the glen and its wildlife in the company of a ranger.

E 🚻 £ D

OS Ref: NN112575
Road: A82, 17m S of Fort William
Bus: Services from Edinburgh, Glasgow and Fort William pass Visitor Centre; Citylink (0870) 505050

Information desk

Self-guided woodland trail

Extensive shop

Café. WiFi available

Baby changing facilities, baby backpacks allowed, easy access for pushchairs on ground floor, regular children's events, children's quiz

Conference facilities available in Maclain Room

Camping (01855) 811397, Easter to 31 Oct (Camping and Caravanning Club)

Audio stories: French, Gaelic, German, Italian, Japanese

Parking at Centre. Visitor Centre, café, shop. Toilets

Objects to handle in Visitor Centre. Four audio stories

Induction loops

Coach/caravan/campervan parking available

5,180ha of land purchased in 1935 and 1937. Achnacon Farm purchased in 1972 to safeguard the amenity. An Torr Woodland purchased in 1993. Inverigan Campsite purchased in 1996

Site	All year		M	T	W	T	F	S	S
Visitor Centre, Shop, Café and Exhibition	3 Jan to 20 Mar	10-4	.	.	.	T	F	S	S
	21 Mar to 31 Oct	9.30-5.30	M	T	W	T	F	S	S
	1 Nov to 15 Dec	10-4	.	.	.	T	F	S	S
	27 Dec to 31 Dec	10-4	M	T	.	.	F	S	S

Last entry to exhibition 45 mins before centre closes.
Contact property or see website for Christmas and New Year opening.

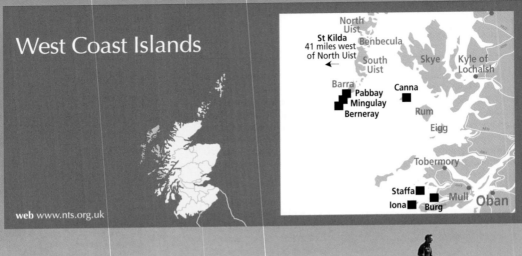

West Coast Islands

North Uist

St Kilda
41 miles west
of North Uist ←

Benbecula

South Uist

Skye

Kyle of Lochalsh

Barra

Pabbay
Mingulay
Berneray

Canna

Rum

Eigg

Tobermory

Staffa

Iona **Burg** Mull

Oban

Burg

Isle of Mull, Argyll & Bute

tel 0844 493 2213

If you want to get away from it all, Burg is a great place to go. Known as 'The Wilderness', this remote corner of south-west Mull is exposed to the full force of the Atlantic weather. But the beautiful wild scenery is also home to important populations of plants and insects, including the rare slender Scotch burnet moth.

Volcanic eruptions many millions of years ago formed the distinctive stepped outline of the peninsula. Although the area is now almost devoid of trees, the sea cliff beyond Burg Farm retains the impression of MacCulloch's fossil tree, engulfed by the lava flow perhaps 50 million years ago.

OS Ref: NM415275
Foot: By footpath, 7m W of Tiroran, off B8035 on north shore of Loch Scridain. Visitors' cars not permitted beyond car park at Tiroran, then a 7m walk on a path which becomes very rough and precipitous, culminating in a steep descent to beach by iron ladder. The fossil tree is not accessible at high tide

Coastal, 7m, exposed in places. Allow 5-6 hours

Dogs must be kept under close control around livestock and cannot negotiate the ladder to the beach

Not advisable due to rough wilderness terrain

569ha bequeathed in 1932 by Mr A Campbell Blair of Dolgelly

Burg	All year	M T W T F S S

Canna

Inner Hebrides

tel 0844 493 2242

A visit to Canna, the most westerly of the Small Isles, is a tonic for the soul. Approaching the island's buttressed cliffs aboard the ferry, there's a sense of the pressures of mainland life slowly releasing their grip. A small farming and crofting community still occupies this tiny island just 4½ miles long and 1 mile wide, while archaeological evidence places people here as far back as the 5th millennium BC.

The 0.8ha Canna House walled garden has been undergoing restoration. Entered through a unique Escallonia tunnel, the garden opens out into lawns, flower borders, an old orchard, soft fruit and a vegetable garden, all being developed to attract bees, butterflies and moths.

OS Ref: NG278050
Ferry: Ferry (no cars) from Mallaig; Caledonian MacBrayne (01475) 650100. Cruises from Mallaig and Arisaig, see page 34

Gille Brighde café restaurant (01687) 460164 www.cannarestaurant.com

Dogs must be kept under close control around livestock

Guided walks; contact property manager

As well as self-catering accommodation, you can stay at Tighard B&B (01687) 462474 www.peaceofcanna.co.uk

Ferry access possible but difficult. Island: hard core gravel roads, assistance required. Tearoom (one step) with picnic tables outside

Canna and the adjacent island of Sanday transferred in 1981 into the Trust's care at the wish of the owner, Dr John Lorne Campbell, who also included his Celtic and Scottish library. St Edward's Church renovated in partnership with the Hebridean Trust to provide a study centre

Canna	All year	M T W T F S S
Canna House	31 Mar to 30 Sep, Wed 1-3; Sat 11-12 & 4-5	
	1 Oct to 31 Mar, Sun 11.30-1.30	

Iona

SW of Mull, Argyll & Bute

tel 0844 493 2214

With its stunning landscape of white sandy beaches and dramatic changing light, Iona is one of the most sacred sites in Britain. It was here in AD 563 that St Columba and his followers arrived from Ireland to spread the gospel throughout Scotland and northern England.

Iona is still a centre for Christian pilgrimage, and its atmosphere of spirituality and the sense of serenity continue to inspire visitors and those who live and work on the island.

OS Ref: NM286240
Ferry: Ferry (no cars) from Fionnphort, Isle of Mull (A849). Ferry to Mull (Craignure) from Oban; Caledonian MacBrayne (01475) 650100. Day excursions in summer, see page 34

(not National Trust for Scotland)

(not National Trust for Scotland)

Dogs must be kept under close control around livestock

Access to ferry by ramp and could be difficult. Access to Abbey along tarmac road (600 metres). Toilet and parking at Fionnphort ferry point

911ha of the island in the care of the Trust since 1979. The Abbey, other sacred buildings and historic sites are not owned by the Trust

Iona	All year	**M T W T F S S**

Mingulay, Berneray and Pabbay

Western Isles

tel 0844 493 2240

Wandering among the abandoned settlements on this remote group of islands is an evocative reminder of those who once lived here. The last of the inhabitants left in 1912, leaving behind a precarious existence based on crofting, fishing and fowling.

Today, Mingulay (12 miles south of Barra) and Berneray are Sites of Special Scientific Interest for the marine vegetation, rock shore and spectacular

cliff habitats found here, as well as a Special Protection Area for the seabird population. All the islands also have significant archaeological sites, with large areas on Mingulay and Pabbay being designated as Scheduled Ancient Monuments.

There are no facilities or services of any kind on the islands. All the islands have very high and dangerous cliffs and landing is difficult.

OS Ref: NL560830

Ranger service between Apr and Sep

Difficult access by boat/launch. No paths on islands, and uneven tracks

Acquired in 2000 with the generous assistance of the Miss J M Fawcitt Bequest, the Chris Brasher Trust, SNH and local support

Mingulay, Berneray, Pabbay	All year	**M T W T F S S**

Staffa >

Staffa National Nature Reserve
W of Mull, Argyll & Bute

tel 0844 493 2215

Despite being only half a mile long and quarter of a mile wide, and completely uninhabited, Staffa has been a source of inspiration for countless visiting artists over the centuries. The island is famous for its distinctive stepped basalt columns, created when the lava from volcanic eruptions cooled many millions of years ago.

These columns form the cathedral-like structure of Fingal's Cave, immortalised by Mendelssohn in his celebrated *Hebrides* overture. Other famous visitors to the island have included Queen Victoria and Prince Albert, the artist J M W Turner, and poets and writers Keats, Wordsworth, Tennyson and Sir Walter Scott.

Staffa is an ideal place to see puffins between May and August.

OS Ref: NM325355
Ferry: 7m W of Mull and 6m NE of Iona. Cruises from Iona, Mull and Oban, see page 34. Landing dependent on suitable weather conditions

Not advisable due to terrain

Ferry accessible with assistance. Steps to top of island and uneven path to Fingal's Cave

Gifted to the Trust in 1986 by John Elliot, Jr, of New York, as an imaginative way to honour the birthday of his wife, Elly. She was honoured with the title Steward of Staffa for her lifetime

Staffa

All year   **M T W T F S S**

Boat tours operate between Apr-Oct (see p34).

Scotland's
National Nature
Reserves

St Kilda World Heritage Site

St Kilda is the most awe-inspiring archipelago in the British Isles. Towering out of the storm-tossed waters of the Atlantic Ocean, its cliffs clamour with the cries of a million seabirds.

St Kilda World Heritage Site
Western Isles

tel 0844 493 2241

Lying 41 miles west of North Uist, St Kilda is home to the largest colony of seabirds in northern Europe, including a quarter of the world's population of northern gannets.

The majestic scenery above water is mirrored by cliffs, caves and reefs plunging into the far depths of the ocean. All teem with carpets of anemones, sponges and other life. This, and the extraordinary clarity of the water, has made St Kilda renowned as one of the foremost dive sites in Europe.

St Kilda is no less famous for its human history. A fragile community clung on for at least 4,000 years in this most remote of places. It's almost unimaginable how the islanders existed in this harsh environment, catching gannets, fulmars and puffins for food, feathers and oil, and farming some meagre crops. A remarkable throwback to the earliest beginnings, the Soay sheep has been preserved on the island almost unchanged in 4,000 years and is one of the most primitive breeds in the world.

The village on the main island of Hirta was laid out in the 1830s and consists of a crescent of houses, each with cultivated plots. These were typical Hebridean single-roomed blackhouses, which the occupants shared with their cattle in winter.

From the mid-19th century the St Kildans began to lose their self-sufficiency, relying more on imports of food, fuel and building materials, and on revenue from tourists. But as contact with the outside world increased, so too did the islanders' dissatisfaction with the realities of life on St Kilda. Finally, on 29 August 1930, the remaining 36 islanders were evacuated to the mainland.

In addition to its dual World Heritage status, St Kilda has been designated a National Nature Reserve, a National Scenic Area, a Site of Special Scientific Interest and a European Community Special Protection Area. The village has been designated a Scheduled Ancient Monument.

OS Ref: NF102991

Ranger service between Apr and Sep

No dogs or other animals are allowed on the islands

Difficult access by boat and launch. Uneven path surfaces

Bequeathed in 1957 by the 5th Marquess of Bute

Scotland's National Nature Reserves

St Kilda	All year	**M T W T F S S**

Ross-shire

Inverewe
Garden & Estate

Ullapool

Poolewe

Corrieshalloch
Gorge

Torridon

Garve

Inverness

Kyle of
Lochalsh

Skye

Falls of Glomach

West Affric

Balmacara
Estate &
Woodland
Walks

Kintail &
Morvich

web www.nts.org.uk

Balmacara Estate & Woodland Walks

Lochalsh House, Balmacara, Kyle, Ross-shire IV40 8DN

tel 0844 493 2233
fax 0844 493 2235
ranger tel/fax 0844 493 2230

How would you like to spend your day? A coastal walk with splendid views across to the Isle of Skye? Strolling among traditional croft lands or native woodlands? Or, for the more active, exploring the coast and offshore islands in a sea kayak? These are just a few of your options when you visit the Balmacara Estate. The area takes in the western end of the Lochalsh peninsula and is criss-crossed with walking trails taking you through native woodland and open moorland to sheltered bays and the pretty crofting villages of Drumbuie, Duirinish and Plockton. And there are also woodland walks through the more exotic policies of Lochalsh House overlooking Loch Alsh. Start your visit at the Balmacara Square Visitor Centre where detailed information is available from a touch-screen display.

OS Ref: NG800278
Road: A87, 3m E of Kyle of Lochalsh **Rail:** Kyle of Lochalsh, Plockton, Duirinish stations

Dogs should be kept under close control at all times

Visitor Centre touch-screen programme: French, Gaelic, German, Italian, Spanish

Parking at the Square. Visitor Centre at the Square accessible with assistance. Other parts inaccessible due to the nature of the terrain

At the Square and other locations throughout the estate

Balmacara Estate bequeathed in 1946 by the late Lady Hamilton. Lochalsh House and policies were conveyed by National Land Fund procedures in 1954

Estate	All year			M T W T F S S
Woodland Walks	All year	9 until dusk		M T W T F S S
Balmacara Square Visitor Centre	29 Mar to 30 Sep	9-5 (Fri 9-4)		M T W T F S S
Plockton Visitor Centre	29 Mar to 20 Oct	11-7		M T W T F S S

Corrieshalloch Gorge National Nature Reserve

Braemore, Ross-shire.
Managed from Inverewe Garden, Poolewe, Ross-shire IV22 2LG

tel 0844 493 2224
fax 0844 493 2226
countryside office tel 0844 493 2224

It's a dizzying and exhilarating experience to look down on the torrent of water plunging 46m (150ft) over the Falls of Measach from the gently swaying suspension bridge. Corrieshalloch Gorge is one of the natural wonders of the Highlands and not to be missed, especially after periods of rain.

The river here has carved a spectacular mile-long box canyon through hard metamorphic rock, and the suspension bridge, built in 1874 to a design by John Fowler, offers the best view of it. Fowler later went on to collaborate on another Scottish landmark – the Forth Railway Bridge.

OS Ref: NH204780
Road: Between A835 (Ullapool road) and A832 (Dundonnell road), 12m SSE of Ullapool. Access from NTS car park on A832 **Bus:** (via stop at Braemore Junction) Scottish Citylink, Inverness to Ullapool, all year; (08705) 505050. Westerbus, Poolewe to Inverness, Mon/Wed/Sat, all year; (01445) 712255. Rapson's Coaches, Ullapool to Gairloch (No 71), Mon-Fri, Apr-Sep; (01463) 710555 **Rail:** Garve, 25m; D&E bus, Gairloch to Inverness (No 35), connects during summer season; (01463) 222444

Based at Inverewe

Care should be taken not to approach the gorge edge, except where indicated

Wheelchair access to viewing point where Loch Broom can be seen. A steep gradient to bridge allows motorised scooter access

14ha given in 1945 by John J Calder of Ardargie. A further 13ha purchased in 1994

Nature Reserve	All year	M T W T F S S

Scotland's National Nature Reserves

Falls of Glomach

Ross-shire

ranger service
tel/fax 0844 493 2230

Walkers who venture out into this far-flung Highland territory are rewarded with a view of one of the highest waterfalls in Britain, at 113m (370ft). The Falls of Glomach are set in a steep narrow cleft in remote country and can only be reached on foot. The best approach is from the Dorusduain car park off the old A87 – a 5-mile walk for which you should allow 5 hours for the round trip. Or, for very fit and experienced walkers, leave the car by the Ling bridge, at the north end of Loch Long, and take the long route along Glen Elchaig before making the steep climb to the Falls. Allow 8 hours for the 7-mile hike.

OS Ref: NH018256
Road: NE of A87, 18m E of Kyle of Lochalsh

Mrs E G M Douglas of Killilan and Capt the Hon Gerald Portman of Inverinate gave 890ha of land in 1941

Falls of Glomach	All year		M T W T F S S

Kintail & Morvich

Morvich Farm, Inverinate, Kyle, Ross-shire IV40 8HQ

tel/fax 0844 493 2231

This magnificent stretch of West Highland scenery is a walkers' paradise. The 7,431ha (18,362a) estate includes the Falls of Glomach (see above) and the Five Sisters of Kintail – four of them over 915m (3,000ft). The best access point to the mountains is the Countryside Centre at Morvich Farm, just off the A87. From April to September the ranger service offers guided walks on Kintail and the Balmacara Estate (see p111). These range from easygoing 2-hour low-level coastal and woodland walks, to challenging all-day mountain walks. Historians take note, the Glenshiel battle site (1719) lies approximately 5 miles east of Shiel Bridge on the A87. An education service for schools is provided, as well as accommodation for groups at the Outdoor Centre at Morvich.

OS Ref: NG961211
Road: N of A87, 16m E of Kyle of Lochalsh **Bus:** daily services from Inverness, Glasgow and Skye

Guided walks – contact ranger service for details

Ranger service offers sea kayaking taster days and more intensive courses

Parking adjacent. Information room in Countryside Centre. No toilet

Purchased in 1944

Estate	All year		M T W T F S S
Countryside Centre at Morvich (unstaffed)	1 Apr to 30 Sep	9am-10pm	M T W T F S S

Torridon

The Mains, Torridon, Achnasheen, Ross-shire IV22 2EZ

tel/fax 0844 493 2228
(Countryside Centre)

With some of the most spectacular mountain scenery in Scotland, Torridon is a magnet for walkers, geologists and naturalists. The estate takes in Liathach, 1,054m (3,456ft) and Beinn Alligin, 985m (3,230ft), composed mainly of Torridonian sandstone dating back 750 million years. Routes to the high tops, and others along the coast, are detailed at the Countryside Centre. You'll also find information about the wildlife on the estate, part of which is in the Beinn Eighe National Nature Reserve. Look out for red deer, grazing Highland cattle, oystercatchers near the sea loch and golden eagles skimming the mountain-tops. If you're very lucky, you may catch sight of a pine marten or otter. The hide near the seashore offers a perfect vantage point for viewing wildlife.

OS Ref: NG906556
Road: N of A896, 10m SW of Kinlochewe **Bus:** Tel 01520 722205 for information

Parking at Countryside Centre. Ramp into Centre. Two steps into Deer Museum. Toilet 55 metres

Torridon Estate (5,611ha) transferred to the care of the Trust by Trustees of the Earl of Lovelace in 1967. A further gift of land at Wester Alligin (827ha) was presented by Messrs B, H and J Blair in 1968, in memory of their parents, Sir Charles Blair Gordon, GBE and Lady Gordon

Scotland's National Nature Reserves

Estate, Deer Enclosure and Deer Museum (unstaffed)	All year		M T W T F S S
Countryside Centre	29 Mar to 30 Sep	10-5	M T W T F . S

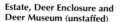

West Affric

Ross-shire

tel/fax 0844 493 2230

This stretch of wild land, linking the Trust's properties at Kintail and Glomach, includes one of the Highland's most popular east-west paths, once part of the drove road from Skye to Dingwall. If you're planning to complete the route, basic accommodation is available at the Alltbeithe Hostel (let to SYHA) and the Camban Bothy (maintained by the Mountain Bothies Association). Throughout the area, the Trust is carrying out vital conservation work to protect the character of this wilderness and restore its natural flora.

OS Ref: NH030180
Bus: In summer from Cannich to Glen Affric car park

At Kintail or Forest Enterprise car park near Affric Lodge, reached from Cannich on A831

Land (3,662ha) purchased in 1993

West Affric	All year	M T W T F S S

Inverewe Garden & Estate

One of the world's great gardens,
Inverewe sprang from the realisation
of one man's determination and
his taste for the exotic. For many,
visiting this beautiful, tranquil place
is an unforgettable experience.

Inverewe Garden & Estate

Poolewe, Ross-shire IV22 2LG

tel 0844 493 2225
fax 0844 493 2227

countryside office
tel 0844 493 2225

Osgood Mackenzie's plan to create a garden from windswept moorland on a rocky peninsula beside Loch Ewe raised a few eyebrows in its day. His vision is still astonishing today, with some of the world's largest growing trees planted into holes hewn out of the bedrock. He chose his site well. The garden is nurtured by the warm currents of the North Atlantic Drift, and is set amidst some of the country's finest scenery.

Over time a kaleidoscope of exotic plants has been cultivated, giving colour and interest throughout the year – a plantsman's paradise with Chinese rhododendrons, Tasmanian eucalypts, Himalayan blue poppies, New Zealand daisy bushes, Chilean lantern-trees, Californian dog's-tooth violets, South African bulbs, Mediterranean rock roses, and many more besides. Here, 'America' and 'Japan' are but a stone's throw apart.

There are also walks leading out from the garden into the surrounding landscape, with its diverse wildlife and spectacular views.

In May 2009 we planted some Wollemi pines *(Wollemia nobilis)* in the Peace Plot area of 'Bambooselem', which we think are the most northerly outdoor collection in the UK. One of the world's rarest plants, these 'fossil trees' were thought to be extinct until discovered in 1994 in a rainforest gorge within the Wollemi National Park in the Blue Mountains of Australia. Fewer than 100 specimens have been found in the wild.

Like its closest living relative, the Monkey Puzzle tree, the Wollemi belongs to the 200 million-year-old *Araucariaceae* family. Its striking, dark green mature leaves – not unlike the spines on a Stegosaur's back – contrast with young, frond-like, apple-green growth, and the black bubbly bark adds to its strange appearance. Unusually for a pine it is naturally multi-stemmed, and long male and round female cones will eventually develop on the same tree. We have chosen a site sheltered from the worst of the winds, so we hope the trees will grow quickly, perhaps reaching 30 metres (100 feet).

🚶 ◻ ❄ ⛩ 🅿 £ C

OS Ref: NG862818 **Road:** On A832, by Poolewe, 6m NE of Gairloch **Bus:** Westerbus, Inverness to Poolewe, Mon-Sat all year; (01445) 712255. D&E Coaches, Inverness to Gairloch (No 35), daily Apr-Sep; (01463) 222444. Rapson's Coaches, Ullapool to Gairloch (No 71), Mon-Fri Apr-Sep; (01463) 710555 **Rail:** Achnasheen station, 35m; D&E Coaches (No 35) connects during season

Free guided walk around garden at 1.30, Mon-Fri, mid-May to early Sep

Pinewood Trail: 30-45 minute walk through hillside plantation adjacent to garden, wonderful views and wildlife interest; some rough terrain, stout footwear advisable; dog friendly. **Kernsary Path:** spectacularly beautiful low-level walk along public right-of-way, leading into upland wilderness of Letterewe estate or returning to Poolewe village via 7m circuit; ground boggy in parts

Licensed self-service restaurant

Baby changing facilities, children's guide

Only assistance dogs allowed in garden. Dog walking area available in adjacent woodland. Pinewood Trail dog friendly. Limited shaded car parking. Two self-lockable cages

Camping Club campsite; (01445) 781249 before 8pm

Guidebook: French, German

Parking at Visitor Centre and restaurant. Visitor Centre, shop, restaurant and some paths in garden accessible. Toilets. Wheelchairs available (pre-booking advisable)

Inverewe Estate (851ha) given by Mairi T Sawyer, daughter of Osgood Hanbury Mackenzie in 1952

Garden and Visitor Centre	28 Mar to 31 May	9.30-5.30		M	T	W	T	F	S	S
	1 Jun to 31 Aug	9.30-6		M	T	W	T	F	S	S
	1 Sep to 30 Sep	9.30-5		M	T	W	T	F	S	S
	1 Oct to 31 Oct	10-4		M	T	W	T	F	S	S
Restaurant	28 Mar to 31 Oct	10-5 (4pm in Oct)		M	T	W	T	F	S	S
Garden only	1 Nov to 31 Mar 2014	10-3		M	T	W	T	F	S	S

The garden may be closed for health and safety reasons in bad weather conditions.

Inverness, Nairn, Moray & the Black Isle

Hugh Miller's Birthplace Cottage & Museum

Cromarty

Brodie Castle

Garve

Nairn

Culloden

Ullapool

Inverness

Kingussie

Brodie Castle

Brodie, Forres, Moray IV36 2TE

tel 0844 493 2156
fax 0844 493 2157

Set in peaceful parkland, this fine 16th-century tower house is packed with enough art and antiques to keep connoisseurs happy all day. It contains fine French furniture; English, continental and Chinese porcelain; and a major collection of paintings, including 17th-century Dutch art, 19th-century English watercolours, and early 20th-century works including paintings by three of the Scottish colourists – Peploe, Cadell and Hunter. The magnificent library contains some 6,000 volumes.

The castle itself was the home of the Brodie family until the late 20th century. In fact, the family's association with the area goes back further than the building of the castle, possibly as far as 1160 when it is believed Malcolm IV gave these lands to the Brodies. In 1645, the castle came under attack from Montrose's army and sustained some damage, but thankfully survived. Today, you can see the additions made to the

building in the 17th and 19th centuries.

Wandering through the grounds these troubled times seem distant indeed, with little to disturb this tranquil setting. In spring, the flowering shrubbery is carpeted with snowdrops, snowflakes and crocuses, followed by massed plantings of daffodils which spill out into the parkland surrounding the castle. The 24th laird, Major Ian Brodie, became a world-renowned breeder of daffodils. Over a hundred of his historic cultivars can be enjoyed in the castle grounds today. You can also stroll by the pond and explore the sheltered woodland walks within the designed landscape, and observe the estate's varied wildlife from the specially constructed hides.

OS Ref: NH980576
Road: Off A96, 4½m W of Forres and 24m E of Inverness **Cycle:** NCN 1
Bus: Stagecoach Bluebird; (01343) 544222

Tearoom

Baby changing facilities, storage for pushchairs, pushchairs ground floor and garden only, children's activities, adventure playground

Civil wedding licence, exclusive dinners, private parties, receptions & marquee areas

Explanatory text: Dutch, French, German, Italian, Spanish, Swedish, Japanese

Parking at castle. Ground floor accessible with assistance (four steps), stairclimber (book in advance) to 1st floor. Woodland paths suitable for wheelchairs and mobility scooters. Toilets. Manual wheelchair available (book in advance)

Castle, its contents and policies (71ha) were taken into the care of the Trust in 1980 through National Land Fund procedures. The late Brodie of Brodie also provided an endowment

Grounds			M T W T F S S
	All year		M T W T F S S
Castle, Tearoom and Shop*	24 Mar to 30 Apr	10.30-4.30	M T W T F S S
	1 May to 30 Jun	10.30-4.30	M T W T . . S
	1 Jul to 31 Aug	10.30-5	M T W T F S S
	1 Sep to 31 Oct	10.30-4.30	M T W T . . S

Last tour starts 1 hour before closing.
Last orders in tearoom 4pm.
* Shop and tearoom open at 11am.

Culloden

Culloden witnessed the darkest day in Scotland's history, with the defeat of Bonnie Prince Charlie's Jacobite army by Government forces.

Culloden

Culloden Moor, Inverness, Highland IV2 5EU

tel 0844 493 2159
fax 0844 493 2160

Culloden Battlefield, scene of the last major battle fought on British soil, is one of the most iconic and emotive sites in Scotland. The course of history changed here on 16 April 1746 and effectively ended Jacobite hopes of restoring the exiled Stuart dynasty to the thrones of Britain. The army of Prince Charles Edward Stuart was crushed by government forces led by the Duke of Cumberland, son of the ruling house of Hanover. The ferocious European war had come to Scotland – dividing families and setting clan against clan.

With over 1,200 dead in just one hour, Culloden was a short but bloody battle. Its outcome was not a foregone conclusion but the odds were stacked against the Jacobites. Stand where the fighting took place and feel the emotion of this brutal battle.

In this world class centre and exhibition there is much to see, experience and learn about Culloden Battlefield. Listen to genuine accounts from characters who were involved in the battle. Their accounts bring the events leading up to and beyond the battle alive. Walk the battlefield, now restored to how it appeared to the opposing forces on that fateful day in 1746. The footpath network enables accessibility for prams, wheelchairs and mobility scooters. The multi-lingual electronic guide, with supporting illustrations, is triggered automatically as you explore the field. The guide uses GPS technology to explain what was happening at strategic points around the battlefield.

Imagine what it was like to be at the centre of the action – a 360° immersive film relives the horror of the battle. Visit the rooftop viewing area to obtain an overall picture of the battlefield and the surrounding area. The animated battle table gives a bird's eye view of the battlefield and the movements of the two armies, and shows how the topography and features on the field contributed to the outcome of the battle. As the clouds part, a narration will help you understand the sequence of events as the battle is re-enacted in front of you using the latest graphic technology. Living History and costumed presentations bring the battle to life.

E ▯ ▮ P

OS Ref: NH745450
Road: B9006, 5m E of Inverness.
Cycle: NCN 1,7 **Bus:** Stagecoach (Nos 2, 2A) from PO, Queensgate, Inverness; 0871 200 2233.
Rail: Inverness station, 6m
Air: Inverness Airport, 7m

→ Electronic battlefield guide

Licensed restaurant, children's menu

Baby changing facilities, children's activities, family tour on battlefield guide

Meeting, workshop and presentation facilities

Dogs permitted in grounds, but we request they are kept on a lead when walking through the battlefield graves area

Multi-lingual battlefield guide device, multi-lingual exhibition leaflet and audio guide

Dedicated accessible parking and toilet. Centre and battlefield DDA compliant. Wheelchair and mobility scooter available

Raised lettering on regimental markers, battlefield guide device automatically triggered as visitor tours battlefield

Induction loop throughout Centre

£ Adult £10, Family £24, 1 parent £20, Concession £7.50

A One hectare at Leanach presented by Alexander Munro in 1937, and his son, John Munro, in 1959. The Graves, Memorial Cairn and King's Stables (1.2ha) presented by Hector Forbes of Culloden in 1944. The Trust purchased the field in which the Cumberland Stone stands in 1945. A further 44.2ha purchased in 1981. The Field of the English (15.5ha) purchased in 1989, and a further 6.3ha of adjacent land purchased in 1998

Site	All year		M T W T F S S
Visitor Centre, Restaurant and Shop	1 Feb to 31 Mar	10-4	M T W T F S S
	1 Apr to 31 May	9-5.30	M T W T F S S
	1 Jun to 31 Aug	9-6	M T W T F S S
	1 Sep to 31 Oct	9-5.30	M T W T F S S
	1 Nov to 23 Dec	10-4	M T W T F S S

Last entry to exhibition and restaurant 30 mins before closing.

Hugh Miller's Birthplace Cottage & Museum

Church Street, Cromarty, Ross-shire IV11 8XA

tel 0844 493 2158

These two very different properties tell the extraordinary story of Hugh Miller's life: Miller House, a handsome Georgian villa built by Hugh's father, and the iconic 17th-century thatched birthplace cottage where Hugh was born in 1802. Beautiful small gardens lie behind both buildings.

The museum in Miller House interprets the life and work of a 'Renaissance man', who rose from humble beginnings as a journeyman stonemason to international renown as one of Scotland's pioneering geologists, and as a crusading newspaper editor. An early folk historian, he also gained fame as an evangelical church reformer. Displays include his outstanding fossil discoveries, manuscripts, shepherd's plaid, mason's mallet and many other artefacts. Touch screens and a hands-on workbench are favourites, especially with younger visitors.

Outside, Miller's Yard is known as a Garden of Wonders because of its many features reflecting natural history. Helen Denerley's remarkable scrap-metal ammonite sculpture is the centrepiece of this delightful garden.

The birthplace is presented through an audio tour taking you round the grounds and interior, with vivid descriptions – many in Hugh's own words – of the building, his ancestors and his own boyhood.

The cottage garden has recently been redesigned and replanted, and has been renamed Lydia Garden in honour of Hugh's wife Lydia, and their descendants.

   D

OS Ref: NH790674
Road: Via Kessock Bridge and A832, in Cromarty, 22m NE of Inverness
Cycle: NCN 1 **Bus:** Rapson's Coaches from Inverness; (01463) 710555

Baby changing facilities, baby backpacks allowed, storage for pushchairs, children's quiz

Coffee and tea available on request

Explanatory text: Dutch, French, German

Free on-street public parking (limited). Ground floor access to cottage only

Access to Miller House ground floor by steps, upper floors by stairs. Cottage has stairs to upper floor; steep steps to garden

Audio tour. Large print exhibition guide

Inductive ear hooks for audio guides

Public parking at shore

Given by Cromarty Town Council in 1938

| Cottage and Museum | 23 Mar to 30 Sep | 12-5 | M T W T F S S |
| | 1 Oct to 31 Oct | 12-5 | . T . T F . . |

Last admission 4.30pm.

Northern Islands

Unst
Yell
Shetland

Orkney
Fair Isle

A836 Thurso

web www.nts.org.uk

Fair Isle

Shetland ZE2 9JU

tel 0844 493 2238

Despite its far-flung location and air of peaceful seclusion, Fair Isle is a hive of industry. The island is famous for its patterned knitwear which is still sold worldwide. Today, the island's craftspeople are also busy with boat-building, spinning and weaving, and the manufacture of furniture and stained-glass windows. The Trust has supported many initiatives to boost the island's economy and prevent depopulation, including a wind-powered renewable energy project. Fair Isle is a birdwatcher's paradise, ideal for studying seabirds and migrating rarities blown here seeking shelter. Other visitors come for the unusual flora and fauna, archaeology, spectacular cliff scenery and traditional crofting practices. The Trust, in partnership with the islanders and the Bird Observatory, is currently working on an important marine protection project.

 OS Ref: HZ210720
Ferry: Regular summer sailings of mail boat, *Good Shepherd IV*, from Grutness, Shetland; Florrie Stout (01595) 760222 **Air:** Flight details: Direct Flight (01595) 840246; from mainland, British Airways (0870) 850 9850

Full board available at South Lighthouse (01595) 760355, Auld Haa Guest House (01595) 760349, Upper Leogh (01595) 760248 and Fair Isle Bird Observatory (01595) 760258. Self-catering at Springfield Croft House (01595) 760225

 Fair Isle and off-lying islands passed to Trust ownership in 1954

Fair Isle	All year	M T W T F S S
Bird Observatory	1 May to 31 Oct	M T W T F S S

Unst & Yell

Shetland ZE2 9UT

tel 0844 493 2239

Located just beyond mainland Shetland, this is the Trust's most northerly estate. It is made up of ten parcels of land, eight of which are on Unst. The smallest is the 12ha (30a) island of Daaey, off Fetlar. The area is of special interest to geologists, botanists and birdwatchers. The three west coast areas of Woodwick, Collaster and Lund offer outstanding scenery, with undulating hills, a low rocky coastline, beaches, cliffs and voes – all typical of Unst. There is an interesting wood – the only one on Unst – at Halligarth, containing mostly sycamores. Most of the land is farmed and the island is also home to a first-class Shetland pony stud.

Ferry: Aberdeen to Lerwick, then (via two ferries) by car or bus to Unst: Northlink Ferries (01856) 885500; John Leask Car Hire (01595) 693162; Inter-island ferries (01595) 743970 **Air:** Loganair (0844) 800 2855 **Travel details:** Lerwick Tourist Information Centre (08701) 999440, or Shetland Council Environment & Transport (01595) 744872

Gifted in 1998 by Joy Sandison

Unst & Yell	All year	M T W T F S S

Little Gems

BALMERINO ABBEY

Balmerino, Fife. Off A914, 5m W of Tay Road Bridge; 10m NW of St Andrews. On NCN 1

Ruins of an impressive Cistercian monastery, founded in 1229 and visited by Mary, Queen of Scots. The monastery building is not accessible but can be viewed from the grounds which provide a tranquil setting, with interesting plants, wildlife and trees including a 400-year-old Spanish chestnut. Guided walks by arrangement.

Given in 1936 by the Earl of Dundee.

BLACK HILL

South Lanarkshire. Off B7018 between Kirkfieldbank and Lesmahagow, 3m W of Lanark

A rich archaeological complex and spectacular viewpoint over the Clyde valley. Site of a Bronze Age burial cairn, an Iron Age hillfort adjoined by a settlement enclosure, and field dykes which may date to the prehistoric and medieval periods. The site was designated a Scheduled Ancient Monument in 1969.

Given in 1936 by Messrs Robert Howie and Sons (2ha).

BOATH DOOCOT

Auldearn, Nairn. Off A96, 2m E of Nairn. 1m from NCN 1

A 17th-century doocot on the site of an ancient motte. Montrose defeated the Covenanters nearby on 9 May 1645; a battle plan is on display.

Given in 1947 by the late Brigadier J Muirhead of Boath, MC.

BRUCE'S STONE

Moss Raploch, Dumfries & Galloway. By A712, 3m W of New Galloway

It is said that King Robert the Bruce rested against this stone after using guerrilla tactics to defeat an English army here in 1307.

Given in 1932 by the Earl of Mar.

BUCINCH & CEARDACH

Loch Lomond

Enquiries to Ben Lomond ranger/naturalist; tel 0844 493 2218.

These two small uninhabited islands, between Luss and Balmaha, were presented by Col Charles L Spencer of Warmanbie, Dumfries, in 1943.

CAIY STANE

Caiystane View, Edinburgh. Off B701, Oxgangs Road. 2m from NCN 75

This impressive 2.7m (9ft) tall prehistoric cup-marked stone, also known as General Kay's Monument, or the Kel Stone, traditionally marks the site of an ancient battle, perhaps between Picts and Romans.

Given in 1936 by Mrs Johnston.

CAMERONIANS' REGIMENTAL MEMORIAL

Douglas, South Lanarkshire. Off A70, 2m W of M74, junction 12. 1m from NCN 74. Bus: Lanark to Douglas

Statue of the Earl of Angus who was the first Colonel of the Cameronian Regiment which was raised at Douglas in 1689. The statue is situated at north edge of the village.

Given with an endowment in 1991 by the Cameronian Trust.

CUNNINGHAME GRAHAM MEMORIAL

Gartmore, Stirling. Off A81, in Gartmore, 2½m SW of Aberfoyle. On NCN 7

Cairn to the memory of R B Cunninghame Graham of Ardoch, distinguished Scottish author, politician and traveller; erected in 1937, one year after his death, at Castlehill, Dumbarton. Moved to Gartmore in 1981.

FINAVON DOOCOT

Angus. Off A90, 6m N of Forfar

Largest doocot in Scotland, with 2,400 nesting boxes. Believed to have been built by the Earl of Crawford in the 16th century.

Passed into the care of the Trust by the Angus Historic Buildings Society in 1993.

MACQUARIE MAUSOLEUM

Gruline, Isle of Mull, Argyll & Bute. Off B8035

The Mausoleum is not Trust property but the Trust has, since 1963, managed it on behalf of the National Trust of Australia (New South Wales). Lachlan Macquarie, who was born nearby at Ulva Ferry in 1761, died in 1824 after distinguished service as Governor of New South Wales and was known as 'the father of Australia'. The Mausoleum is on the Gruline estate, which he owned.

MURRAY ISLES

Dumfries & Galloway. Near Gatehouse of Fleet, off A75. Near NCN 7. Accessible only by boat. Please do not visit during bird breeding season, May-July

Two small uninhabited islands in the Islands of Fleet, Wigtown Bay, off Carrick Point. The islands are host to a colony of cormorants and are significant as a site for breeding gulls.

Given in 1991 by Mrs Murray Usher, OBE.

SHIELDAIG ISLAND

Torridon, Ross-shire. In Loch Torridon. Off Shieldaig, A896

The island is almost entirely covered in Scots pine, thought to have been planted over 100 years ago to provide poles for drying the nets of local fishermen. The island is still a haven for wildlife as herons use the trees for nesting platforms, and seals haul themselves out of the water onto the rocky foreshore.

Purchased in 1970.

STROME CASTLE

Ross-shire. Off A896, 4½m SW of Lochcarron

This ruined castle is romantically situated on a rocky promontory jutting into Loch Carron, commanding fine views westwards to Skye. First recorded in 1472 when it was a stronghold of the Lords of the Isles, it later belonged to the MacDonnells of Glengarry. Following a quarrel with Kenneth MacKenzie, Lord of Kintail, it fell in 1602 after a long siege and was blown up.

Given in 1939 by Mr C W Murray.

TIGHNABRUAICH VIEWPOINT

Argyll & Bute. On A8003, NE of Tighnabruaich

The indicators, attributed to the Trust and the Scottish Civic Trust, were erected by a Trust supporter in memory of two brothers, who gave generously of their time to the work of the Trust.

VENNIEHILL

Gatehouse of Fleet, Dumfries & Galloway. Off A75. 1m from NCN 7

1.4ha (3.5a) of wildflower-rich grassland with a hilltop viewpoint, at the west end of the main street, managed to encourage diversity of flora and associated invertebrates. The hilltop is partially surrounded by a low earthwork, perhaps the defence structure of an old fort or early settlement.

Given in 1981 by Mrs Murray Usher, OBE.

Properties owned by the National Trust for Scotland and under guardianship agreements or leased to others

ANTONINE WALL
Three sections along B816, W of Falkirk.

The Wall was built from the Forth to the Clyde about AD 142 and consisted of ditch, turf rampart and road, with forts every 2 miles. One of the Trust's sections includes Rough Castle, 3 miles west of Falkirk, the best preserved of the forts. Gifted by Kerse Estates, Mr C W Forbes of Callander in 1938.

In the care of Historic Scotland.

Open: All year

CASTLE CAMPBELL
Off A91, N of Dollar, Clackmannanshire. Tel 01259 742408

Built in the late 15th century, this was once the home of the chief of Clan Campbell. John Knox is said to have preached here in the 16th century. Presented to the Trust in 1950 by Mr J E Kerr of Harviestoun.

In the care of Historic Scotland.

Open: 1 Apr to 30 Sep, daily 9.30-5.30; 1 Oct to 31 Mar, daily 9.30-4.30 (Oct-Mar closed Thu-Fri)

Free entry for NTS members.

CASTLEHILL
On A814, in Dumbarton.

1.6ha (4a) let to West Dunbartonshire Council. Given to the Trust in 1936 by Captain Angus Cunninghame Graham RN.

Open: All year

CLAVA CAIRNS
Off B9091, 5m E of Inverness, Highland. Tel 01667 460232

Dating from around 2000 BC, these circular burial chambers are surrounded by standing stones. The cairns are among the most outstanding Scottish prehistoric monuments. Interpretation boards on site. Gifted in 1945 by J G Murray of Culloden.

In the care of Historic Scotland.

Open: All year

CROOKSTON CASTLE
Brockburn Road, 4m SW of Glasgow city centre. Tel 0141 883 9606

Early 15th-century tower house on the site of a 12th-century castle. Mary, Queen of Scots and Darnley stayed here after their marriage in 1565. Gifted in 1931 by Sir John Stirling Maxwell, Bt, it was the Trust's first property.

In the care of Historic Scotland.

Open: All year, daily 9.30-4.30 (Oct-Mar closed Thu-Fri)

DIRLETON CASTLE
On A198, in Dirleton, East Lothian. Tel 01620 850330

Beautiful ruins dating back to 1225, with 14th/16th-century additions. The castle has had an eventful history, from its first siege by Edward I in 1298 until its destruction in 1650. The garden encloses a late 16th-century bowling green surrounded by yew trees. Sales kiosk and exhibition. Gifted in 1981 by Vice-Admiral B C E Brooke.

In the care of Historic Scotland.

Open: 1 Apr to 30 Sep, daily 9.30-5.30; 1 Oct to 31 Mar, daily 9.30-4.30

Admission charged. Please call for prices.

GLENLUCE ABBEY GLEBE
2m NW of Glenluce, Dumfries & Galloway. Tel 01581 300541

Part of the glebe adjoining Glenluce Abbey, a ruined Cistercian abbey founded by Roland, Lord of Galloway, in 1192. Purchased by the Trust in 1933.

In the care of Historic Scotland.

Open: 1 Apr to 30 Sep, daily 9.30-5.30

Admission charged. Please call for prices.

Properties owned by the National Trust for Scotland and under guardianship agreements or leased to others

PARKLEA FARM
A8, off M8, 1m E of Port Glasgow, Inverclyde.

A strip of 27ha (68a) of land on the south bank of the Clyde, leased at a nominal rent to Inverclyde Council as a recreation ground. Bought from a bequest by Norman P Anderson in 1949.

Open: All year

PRESTON TOWER
Off A198, Prestonpans, East Lothian.

Adjacent to Hamilton House, Preston Tower was built by the Hamilton family in the 15th century. It was burned by Cromwell in 1650, then rebuilt with Renaissance additions on top. Also, 17th-century doocot and wall. Purchased by the Trust in 1969.

Managed by East Lothian Council.

Open: All year

PROVAN HALL
Auchinlea Road, Easterhouse, Glasgow G34 9QN.

Built in the 15th century, this is probably the most perfect pre-Reformation mansion house in Scotland. Given to the Trust in 1938.

Now part of Auchinlea Park, the property is managed by Glasgow City Council.

Open: All year, Mon-Fri 9-4.30 (except 25/26 Dec and 1/2 Jan and when special events are in progress)

PROVOST ROSS'S HOUSE
(Aberdeen Maritime Museum) Shiprow, Aberdeen AB11 5BY.
Tel 01224 337700

Built in 1593, Provost Ross's House is the third oldest house in Aberdeen. In 1952, when in danger of demolition, the house was acquired from the Town Council, together with a substantial donation. It now houses part of the Aberdeen Maritime Museum, operated by the City of Aberdeen Council, which gives a wonderful insight into the rich maritime history of the city.

Open: All year, Tues-Sat 10-5, Sun 12-3

SCOTSTARVIT TOWER
Off A916, 2½m S of Cupar, Fife.

Situated three-quarters of a mile west of Hill of Tarvit Mansionhouse, this fine tower was known to have existed in 1579. Gifted, together with neighbouring Hill of Tarvit, by Miss E C Sharp in 1949.

In the care of Historic Scotland.

Open: Summer only. Call 01786 431324 for access details.

THREAVE CASTLE
3m W of Castle Douglas, Dumfries & Galloway. Tel 07711 223101

This 14th-century Douglas stronghold stands on Threave Island in the River Dee. Gifted in 1948, together with neighbouring Threave House and Garden, by Major A F Gordon DSO, MC.

In the care of Historic Scotland.

Open: 1 Apr to 31 Oct, daily 9.30-5.30 (4.30pm in Oct). Last outward sailing 4.30pm (3.30pm in Oct).

Admission charged to non-NTS members. Please call for prices.

URQUHART CASTLE
On A82, on Loch Ness, near Drumnadrochit. Tel 01456 450551

One of Scotland's iconic landmarks, Urquhart Castle, on the banks of Loch Ness, remains an impressive stronghold despite its ruinous state. Once one of Scotland's largest castles, the remains include a tower house that commands splendid views of the famous loch and Great Glen. Gifted by Mrs Eila Chewett in 2004.

Managed by Historic Scotland.

Open: 1 Apr to 30 Sep, daily 9.30-6; Oct, daily 9.30-5; 1 Nov to 31 Mar, daily 9.30-4.30. Last ticket sold 45 mins before closing.

Admission charged. Please call for prices.

If you would like to find out about Conservation Agreements or properties which are owned by the Trust but not open to the public, please visit www.nts.org.uk

A place for celebrations

For information about holding your event at a Trust property call 0844 493 2111; email functions@nts.org.uk or visit www.nts.org.uk.

Photographers

Index